Healing Is For Real

This book is dedicated to
my father,
Harold Edson Miner, M.D.,
my mother,
Blanche Temple Miner, R.N.,
and
my brother,
Philip Barton Miner, M.D.
Co-workers with me in the
Healing Ministry

HEALING IS FOR REAL

by

Malcolm H. Miner

MOREHOUSE-BARLOW CO.
Wilton, Connecticut

Fourth printing, 1979
Copyright © 1972 by Morehouse-Barlow Co.,
78 Danbury Road, Wilton, Connecticut 06897
Library of Congress Catalog Number 72-80884
Standard Book Number 0-8192-1132-X
Printed in the United States of America

Contents

Preface

I.   Healing: A Normal Part of Christian Living   11

II.   It Won't Hurt Any   17

III.   But Not All Are Healed   24

IV.   We Know So Little About It   36

V.   Healing is Loving   46

VI.   Healing is Forgiving   53

VII.   Mental and Emotional Illness   62

VIII.   God's Anesthesia   71

IX.   Varieties of Healing Experiences   75

X.   Who Can Be Healed?   87

XI.   Where Do We Go From Here?   96

XII.   You Can Heal   111

Footnotes   121

Bibliography   124

Preface

I had to ask myself one question as I started to write this book on spiritual healing. By what authority do I write these things? I am not a doctor of medicine, nor do I possess graduate degrees in psychology or psychiatry. I do not hold a chair in a university, nor am I on the faculty of a theological seminary. However, I do feel that I have something to say that is relevant to our times, for we live in a world in which sickness is seen not only in matters of organic disease—but perhaps more in the areas of human relationships.

As an Episcopal priest, ordained to serve Christ in the "One, Holy, Catholic and Apostolic Church," I am a man under orders; in the carrying out of those orders I have witnessed the wonderful works of God in the form of healing. I have observed the whole panorama of healing in its many varieties, forms and shapes as applied to organic disease, emotional and mental illness, spiritual attrition and other forms of blight in man as an individual, as well as in people as they cluster and have an identity in groups.

Concerning medicine and health, I have always had more than a passing acquaintance with the subject from the earliest days of childhood when, as a doctor's son, I grabbed up all the "Mentholatum" samples that came in the mail and established a rather good medical practice of my own at the age of five. During my high school days I was the kid who made the citrate of magnesia and tended the fountain at the local pharmacy. In later years I worked as a representative for a pharmaceutical company, again in active association with doctors, pharmacists and hospitals. However, it is obvious that with such experience alone I should never have come to write this book. The authority by which I write is the same authority that gives me the right to preach and to teach: to baptize, to celebrate the Holy Communion, to anoint and lay hands upon the sick, to pronounce the absolution and to give the blessing. It is the authority given to me by Christ through my bishop, when he laid hands upon me at my ordination.

So it is by that authority that I dare to write these things. "For we cannot but speak the things which we have seen and heard (Acts 4:20). Following the direction of the Holy Spirit I have been led to different places where I have served in different ways. I have always served a parish, but also I have served as a college chaplain, as a missionary, and as a city councilman. In all of those varying experiences the healing power of God made its presence known.

I have served the Church in "Jerusalem, and in all Judaea, and in Samaria, and unto the uttermost part of the earth" (Acts 1:8) and everywhere I have gone I have experienced the gifts of healing. This is my witness.

Malcolm H. Miner

Healing Is For Real

I.
Healing: A Normal Part of Christian Living

As the man says, "healing is for real." I didn't always have this belief about healing through prayer or other spiritual means. In fact, I was more stubborn than most about accepting what should have been obvious to me: the fact that prayer works, and that by faith the sick are healed. I have laid hands upon a head covered with ugly bumps and have seen those bumps disappear within minutes. I have stood over a sick baby so filled with congestion he could hardly breathe and, after prayer and the touch of my hand, have watched the instant change as he began to breathe clearly and his fever left. Yes, in the face of these and many other similar experiences I have come to say with conviction that "healing is for real."

I have come to understand healing as a by-product of Christian living through my personal experience in the parish ministry. I am convinced that God constantly brings about healing in different forms and degrees in the regular living of the Christian faith. He does this often and without fanfare, and His power is available to us at any time. We are all called to share in this ministry of healing. One does not have to possess a special gift of healing to share in this ministry. God can and will use any one of us to bring His healing grace to the sick.

It is not my purpose to prove anything to you. The cases I shall mention are not scientifically documented, but the situations are real. These things happened in my presence as I practiced a normal ministry. I am not one who has made a specialty of healing, but rather a parish priest who has found healing to be an integral part of total ministry. I have found myself involved constantly in a healing ministry, without any great effort on my own part. It is because I have experienced healing in myself, and in my own family, among parishioners and strangers—it is because of these personal encounters with what Agnes Sanford calls God's "healing light"—that I know it to be readily available to others. I am convinced that you, too, may accept this and believe it when it is, likewise, born of your personal experience. In the telling of my story I shall try to lead you to an awareness of these possibilities in your own life and in your own ministry—for every Christian has a ministry. It is possible to be surrounded by God's healing powers in yourself and in others and still not be aware of it, but I am confident that one cannot carry on a normal Christian Ministry without finding healing as a by-product of that ministry. It is impossible to pray without receiving some kind of results. Even when you are not attempting to release God's healing powers, the actions, faith, and prayers of those to whom you minister will have their effect. While all others have given up on a dying person some small child's anonymous prayer sets the healing chain in motion—and the patient recovers.

Due to the persistence of healing in various ways that I have encountered over and over again—healings when my faith was strong, healings when my faith was weak, long term healings of mind and soul, instantaneous healings of bodily illness, healings by phone, healings requested and those unsolicited, *because of all these things*—I have become deeply sensitive to God's presence and power in our midst today.

We are simply too academic in our approach to God in this age and we have become insensitive to God's availability and nearness. We believe that God is many things and we can spend the whole evening discussing His nature in an objective manner, but we're scared to death to be subjective about Him because that's too personal. That means that we'd have to believe *in* Him rather than *about* Him, and that would involve commitment. That would involve *faith,* even faith in miracles, *even faith in healing.*

It is precisely because I have been a normal twentieth-century churchman—trained to be objective, brought up to question, difficult to convince—that my experiences may be relevant to many. Bombarded on every side with evidences of God's healing in those around me, I could still speak only in cautious terms—often a typical clerical attitude in these matters. Brought up as the son of a physician and a nurse, I was accustomed to thinking of healing in purely medical terms: doctors, nurses, hospitals, medicines, X-rays, surgery. Yet, neither my father nor my mother ever taught me that. I just took it for granted that if someone was sick it was a matter for the doctor . . . period. Even as a seminarian and later, at the beginning of my ministry, I looked upon prayer for the sick as a good thing, a psychologically sound thing, but not really an effective means of healing, except in rare cases. I still feel that a physician should be seen in times of sickness, for God usually uses those engaged in the field of medicine to bring about His healing in others. That does not, however, rule out prayer or spiritual healing.

As a seminarian I was thrown off balance abruptly when a crippled lady fired this question at me: "Do you heal the lame?" At that time in my life I was quite unprepared to discuss the possibilities of spiritual healing in her case and in others; not quite knowing what to say, I replied, "I haven't gone that far yet." As I look back at that experience, having been a witness to many wonderful healings in the years that followed, I realize that my answer to the lady was more prophetic than I knew at the time. How true those words, "haven't gone that far yet," diagnosed my position then. For a vital conviction concerning spiritual healing, I hadn't lived long enough, hadn't experienced God's power in that way, had not matured in my faith enough to let Him use me as an instrument for His healing in others.

My first impressive experience with prayer as an active means of healing came about quite naturally in the course of my work in the ministry. Late one night I was notified by my doctor, who was also my parishioner and friend, that one of our church members was dying: "If you want to see her alive, you'd better get right over here . . . she's in a coma and is failing fast. I don't expect she'll last until morning."

When I arrived, her daughter, a woman in her thirties, informed me that her mother was in a coma, but surprised me by asking me to pray for her recovery. It seemed a little late for that, but I did not express the thought aloud. Already been given up by the doctor, a woman with a history of heart disease, and now in a coma—it seemed to me that we were almost asking too much of God . . . after all. As her priest, however, I couldn't refuse the request. It certainly wouldn't do any harm to ask for God's help, and close the prayer with "Thy will be done."

I approached the bedside of the unconscious woman and, laying hands upon her head, I prayed, "Most merciful Father, heal this Thy servant in mind, body, and soul, through Jesus Christ our Lord. Amen." Just as soon as I concluded this short prayer the sick woman's daughter added, "Thank God, thank God." I'm so glad you came, and thank you for the prayer. I know mother's going to be all right now."

I'm sorry to say that I didn't share her confidence in my prayer, though I did feel my presence there was a help to the young woman. Her attitude confirmed my belief that even if the prayers didn't help the mother, who was in a coma and unable to respond, they did give strength and psychological support to the grieving daughter. I went home fully expecting to be called the next day to make arrangements for a funeral.

I did receive a call the next morning about seven-thirty. It was the doctor.

"What did you do to my patient when you were here last night?"

"Do? I just said a prayer for her recovery. Why?"

"Well, it must have been one of your very special prayers, with a gold frame around it. Our patient has recovered—she's all better!"

"What do you mean, 'she's all better'," I probed further in my astonishment, "You mean she's out of the coma?"

"Out of the coma, yes! I mean *all better*—like doing the shopping next week."

When I had a chance to talk with the recovered patient and her daughter I learned what had happened between my visit late at night and the doctor's visit the next morning.

"As soon as you left, my mother came to. She sat up and looked around, and touching her head, she asked me who had been here. I said, 'Father Miner . . . he said a prayer for you.' Then Mamma said, 'I'm hungry, I'd like something to eat.' She looked real good and I asked her how she felt and she said, 'Just fine—I feel just fine.' And then I looked at her . . . and tears came into my eyes and a lump in my throat . . . and I *knew* she was well. God had answered our prayers. Then the doctor came by in the morning and, well, he couldn't believe it. He kept shaking his head and saying that over and over. He'd take out his stethoscope and listen to her heart, then he'd look at me and say, 'I can't believe it—I just can't believe it'!"

To me, at that point in my ministry, it was as dumbfounding as it was to the doctor. I thought of it as a very interesting phenomenon, but I was not sure of what I had contributed to that healing. I was still hesitant about accepting it as a natural result of faith and prayer. But the experience did make me think. Though I was not ready to recognize it as one of God's miracles, neither was I ready to treat it as a mere coincidence.

I continued to ask myself, "Was it really a miraculous healing? Did my prayer and the laying-on-of-hands have anything to do with this amazing recovery? Was it the daughter's faith that brought it about?"

After sharing in that vital experience I went back to my routine duties in the parish—the church school, the youth program—attending to the social and religious activities of the congregation. I soon forgot how overwhelming the experience had been—and so did everyone else who had heard of it. They remembered how sick Mrs. B. had been and how she recovered so suddenly. It was not a matter of the good news to be shouted from the housetops, but rather just an interesting thing that had happened to a friend. I continued to see the sick and to pray for them—and most recovered, and some quite dramatically—but I was too reserved or insecure to fully accept it as spiritual healing. Yes, I went back to my normal parish routine where I have stayed throughout my ministry—but the door had been opened. I was ready to entertain the possibility of spiritual healing as the result of faith and prayer, and in time I was to be convinced of it.

II.
It Won't Hurt Any

"Say a prayer if you want—it won't hurt any."

What clergyman hasn't heard that line while calling on the sick? The statement reveals a common judgment on spiritual healing in our times. Our generation has been taught to rely solely upon medical men in all matters pertaining to health. Prayer, if it's used at all, is looked upon as an extra coating, thrown in for good measure—a little added insurance—"it won't hurt any."

Because of the complex nature of man it is not easy to measure the exact relative effects of a dosage of medicine, a session of psychiatric counseling, and a spiritual ministration such as the laying-on-of-hands or anointing. In my opinion, however, a person who receives spiritual ministrations usually does better in all areas of mind, body, and spirit. The doctor will be pleased to hear that his patient has responded so well to the drug or surgery, as the case may be. If counseling has been employed, the counselor will remark about the patient's improved attitude and the remarkable progress that's been made. And, if the patient is knowledgeable in matters of spiritual healing, he knows the reason for his remarkable response in those other areas.

Even if a patient doesn't realize the part prayer has played in his recovery, I do—because over and over I have witnessed this same thing, have heard similar remarks about the unusually good progress, whether it is the overcoming of an infection, recovery from surgery, or the mending of a broken bone. In my ministry to the sick these elements have been common: the reduction or absence of pain (even when considered normal to the condition), the rapid healing of the patient, and the positive mental attitude of the sick person. Where I have ministered in conjunction with the same physicians, they have come to have respect for spiritual therapy and have welcomed, even requested, my participation.

Because everybody is accustomed to looking for the big miracle, the dramatic experience of a healing at Lourdes or from the pages of the New Testament, much of the value of healing prayer is overlooked or unrecognized. The dramatic experience is usually believed by most people, but it is a miracle far removed from the average person's experience. He has read of these things—has heard of them, can tell you of some distant relative who had a remarkable recovery—but in general thinks of them as exceptions to the rule. So we continue to look for the big miracle, ignoring the many opportunities for spiritual healing in every kind of illness we face daily in our lives. We continue to be dependent upon stomach remedies, headache remedies, and tranquilizers in everyday matters of health, believing that God can cause the lame to walk, the deaf to hear and the blind to see, but doesn't do much for an acid stomach or a sinus headache.

Children have not always had time to learn doubt in the these matters and, as a result, have often demonstrated to me the constant availability of God's healing power in these common ailments. My own children, having been reared with an awareness of prayer as a means of healing, regularly came to me when they had colds, sore throats, earaches, and other conditions, asking for the laying-on-of-hands. Not only did they come themselves, but often they brought their friends to me to receive prayers for various ailments. I might have been reading the newspaper or otherwise engaged, it never seemed to be a planned arrangement. They would just walk up to me and say, "Dad, Bill has an awful cold and his chest hurts. Will you give him the laying-on-of-hands?" It might be Cathy with an earache or Sandy with a headache, but it was always considered the right thing for them to do in all cases of illness. When they came to me I would ask them their problem, then, usually laying hands on them, I would say a short prayer and send them on their way again. Most of the time those kids took it for granted that healing would take place and, as a matter of fact, it usually did. For them it was as effective and just as ordinary as it would have been to receive an injection of penicillin from their doctor, and much less painful.

In our church it is customary for me to lay hands upon those who are sick at a midweek service. Often pre-school children accompany their parents to the service, which is held in the morning. Once, after putting up with a long siege of coughing and noseblowing on the part of her mother, a little four-year-old finally spoke her mind on the subject: "If I were as sick as you seem to be I'd go down to the church and get a shot from Father Miner."

In her mind the efficacy of the laying-on-of-hands was at least on a par with treatment received at the hands of a physician. While I am not advocating spiritual healing as a replacement for doctors and medicine, I am sure that our little friend made a good point. Prayer therapy is available to us at all times and can and should be used by all of us before making that appointment with the doctor. If we always tried prayer first, perhaps we should make fewer appointments with the physician. Too often we completely ignore the possibilities of prayer in matters of health. A person has to be practically dying before someone thinks to add his name to the prayer list. The mother of this child was a good Christian woman who believed in spiritual healing and often had intercessory prayer for others. But, in her own misery with cold and flu, she didn't even think of spiritual healing as applied to herself—until her child spoke. Jesus said, "Believe me . . . unless you change your whole outlook and become like little children you will never enter the kingdom of Heaven" (Matthew 18:3, Phillips).

There are those who feel that spiritual healing is only of value in illnesses of a psychosomatic nature, that is physical disorders which originate in mental or emotional processes. They say that spiritual healing is this same process in reverse: that instead of causing illness in the body, spiritual therapy heals a condition which has been mentally induced. Certainly that is true to a degree, for we are not just bodies, not just minds, not just souls, but are made up of all three. As a result, we cannot rule out the value of positive thinking in health any more than we can rule out the value of proper exercise, proper diet, and sufficient sleep.

Our attitude of mind sets our response mechanism in a positive or negative direction. Naturally, if we think positively we help the natural healing in our bodies to function better, for our thoughts are cooperating with the antibodies and other agents within us whose job it is to keep us well. As soon as a virus or bacterium enters our system, God's healing substances in our bodies go to work to combat the alien germ. Other changes take place: the white blood count goes up, our body temperature rises, as our whole being becomes involved in driving out the disruptive influence and restoring up to good health again.

A negative attitude triggers a like response in our built-in healing mechanism. You say, "I know I'm going to catch a cold," and you are telling the antibodies that it's no use for them to try to prevent it for it's a losing cause—so you get a cold. Your mind has already made the decision that you are going to get a cold, and it must not "lose face," so the body works hard to oblige. That is true whether you are thinking positively or negatively. The body will always do its best to accommodate the mind. This is why it is so important to push back negativity whenever it appears in your thinking.

In all of his writings Glen Clark makes a strong point of

avoiding negativity in all matters of both one's personal health as well as healing in others. In his book, *Be Thou Made Whole,* he suggests preventive measures which would not allow negativity to get in your way:

> People who are so full of Love, Joy, Peace, and Trust that there is no room in them for negative emotions to enter are the people who always keep well. They are also the people who can become splendid instruments for the healing of others.[1]

When doubt and fear find their way into the picture, a dark cloud hovers over the sickroom, and that gloom infects the people who surround the patient—the nurses, the family members and close friends—and the patient himself.

I am reminded of a young boy who had been given up by practically everyone following surgery involving the removal of a section of his intestines. There is a saying, "the operation was a success but the patient died," and it seemed as though that would be the case. The operation was a success but the tissues were not mending well. His body was rejecting all food, solid and liquid, and as long as passage through his intestines was impossible, hope was very dim for the boy's survival. He grew weaker day by day. The parents were prepared for the worst. All seemed hopeless when I felt a strong urge to go to his bedside late one Saturday night. As I entered the room his special nurse left, and as she passed by I could see that she had tears in her eyes. I moved close to his still form and spoke to him.

"Hi, Pal, I just came by to have a little talk with you—and to say a prayer for you, O.K.?"

"O.K., Father," he answered with a trace of a smile forming on his lips.

"Do you know why I want to pray for you?"

"So God will make me well again."

"Do you think God can make you well again?"

"Sure God can make me well again. God can do anything He wants."

"Do you think if I pray for you God will heal you soon?"

"I really think so."

"So do I."

Then I asked him to close his eyes as I laid my hands on his head and offered prayers anew for his recovery. He went to sleep instantly, but I remained by his side for quite some time as I continued to pray silently. In the morning wonderful things began to happen. He called out to the nurse asking for breakfast. He hadn't eaten solids since his operation, in fact, he had not been able to hold liquids. But this morning he ate his entire breakfast and it passed through his intestines normally. Right away his strength began coming to him. In two days he was out of bed, walking around the room. In a week's time he was to be discharged from the hospital. This was hardly a case of psychosomatic illness, but certainly this young patient's own positive attitude allowed God's natural healing power to go to work and the saying to go like this: "The operation was a success *and the patient lived*."

Naturally, this was a time of great rejoicing for all connected with the little fellow and his close call: his doctor, nurses, parents, and friends. Still, at the very moment when his life was at its lowest ebb, there were many who would have said upon seeing me there, "Sure, say a prayer if you'd like to . . . it won't hurt any."

I said my prayer, asking the patient to let God help him by merely being receptive to that help, to steer his mind in a positive direction, the direction of light, hope, and health. As the case often had been before, the beautiful experience of spiritual healing was witnessed by many.

At a time like that the minds of those witnesses are suddenly made aware that it is not only only true that prayer "won't hurt any"; in reality prayer helps immeasurably. The problem is that those who have witnessed a specific healing tend to treat it as a once in a lifetime occurrence; they don't look expectantly for the healing of others around them who are sick.

Once our eyes have been opened to the possibilities available to us through spiritual resources, we should not hesitate to use them daily in our lives. We should make intercessory prayer a regular part of our routine each morning and evening. When we learn that someone is ill, is expecting surgery, is anxious or upset in mind, body, or spirit, then we should pray for them. I assure you—it helps.

III.
But Not All Are Healed

One of the most common fears about praying for the sick and their recovery is the fear of failure.

"Suppose you pray for him and he doesn't get better? He'll think that God has let him down. Or suppose he dies—then what do you tell the family?"

Yes, these are all legitimate questions to ask. But don't these same questions face the surgeon as he prepares to operate? What doctor do you know who has a perfect record of cures? None. Yet, in the face of failure many times in the past, the physician works with each patient individually, doing his very best to restore each one to health.

We must have the same conviction that the doctor has: knowing that health and wholeness are possible in the sick person, and that if a cure is not realized this time, perhaps success will be achieved in the next patient. We know, like the doctor, that God can heal the sick, regardless of the condition; with that belief in mind we should have the same courage as the medical man to do all in our power to bring about healing. The fact that we cannot see an outward healing does not give us the right to stop trying. Also, the absence of an outward healing does not mean that there hasn't been an inward healing of mind or soul.

Those who question the forthright approach to spiritual healing forget that Jesus instructed His disciples to go and heal with just as much authority as He sent them forth to baptize and to preach the "good news." He didn't say to give up all efforts at spiritual healing if your first effort seems to have failed. Nothing of the kind! He sent them forth to heal the sick—and that same command applies to his followers today.

The matter of obedience to our Lord's commands is taken up in depth by Bernard Martin in his book, *The Healing Ministry in the Church,* Martin carefully documents the Biblical evidence that presents the healing ministry as a response to the directives of Jesus Christ.

> If, therefore, the Church really seeks to live and act "in the name of Jesus," in whom she believes and whom she recognizes as Head, she cannot ignore the signs promised to those who believe. The Christian healing ministry does not consist in the first place in seeking for individual gifts of healing, such as were made manifest from the beginning and throughout the history of the Church, but rather in obeying commands given by the Lord for the whole Church which constitutes His Body. And it is as a result of this willing obedience to definite commands as well as in the faith in the visible manifestation of the divinity of Jesus Christ that the Holy Spirit will give certain particular gifts, if it be the will of God.[1]

A healing ministry works to carry out those commands, to do what we know about healing the sick—to pray, to give the laying-on-of-hands, to anoint with oil, to offer Christ's forgiveness and the Holy Communion, to call upon the resources of the prayer group—all in cooperation with the doctor who is assigned to the case. The healing minister's job is to carry our orders, not to make a judgment on the healing response in the sick person.

All who have worked with the sick have come to realize that there are different kinds of healings and different degrees of healing. Previously mentioned was the belief in the big miracle, the complete and sudden healing of one hopelessly ill. Because we tend to think of spiritual healing in that vein it is easy to overlook healing as it is seen in lesser degrees, or healing which is primarily of the mind or spirit. These healings are among the most significant ones, because of the profound spiritual growth and comprehension apparent in the sick person. In many cases the patient becomes the one who is ministering to the would-be comforters. All members of the clergy have been ministered to by those they sought to help.

One such person from whom I received help was the victim of a long siege of cancer of the bone. When I first knew him he was ambulatory and the only treatment he was receiving was X-ray therapy. He had been brought up in the Church but had grown away from its fellowship. We became friends and as his illness progressed I continued to minister to him. I prayed for him and brought him the sacrament of Holy Communion on a regular schedule. Then he began to demonstrate a sudden growth spiritually, reminiscent of the prayer which asks that "the more the outward man decayeth, strengthen him, we beseech thee, so much the more continually with thy grace and Holy Spirit in the inner man."[2] Progressively, as his body grew weaker his mind and spirit grew in grace, until the very love of God radiated from his personality. He could feel it happening to himself. He said that his new closeness to God came from his frequent receptions of the Eucharist and our healing prayers, offered daily. The sacrament nurtured his soul and the laying-on-of-hands eased his bodily pain. With sick people it is often the long nights which are so difficult to take, but these were made easier by our ministrations.

"I feel at peace for the whole night after you've put your hands on my head and prayed."

Finally, my friend died, confidently, peacefully, courageously, giving a benediction to his whole family gathered around. Are we to call that a failure? I say he was *healed*.

The conservative attitude toward spiritual therapy on the

part of some of the clergy comes from the recognition that not all people respond to it in the same way: some are suddenly and dramatically healed, some are improved or healed partially, and some get worse and die. Anyone who has ministered to the sick on a regular basis has seen these differences in response to the same ministrations, essentially. The same thing is true of participants in healing service: some are obviously healed, some apparently are not. Because we cannot guarantee a specific response to healing prayer, some ministers feel that they must approach the sick with caution, leaving the whole matter to the will of God.

I do not think it is right to suggest to a sick person that he is in that condition because God wants him to suffer. While it is true that God allows us to suffer, and even gain benefit from that suffering, I do not believe He wills us to suffer. We are free to move as we please as God's children, and as free agents we may sin and may also become subject to other ungodly conditions such as disease. Part of being free is being subject to hazards which confront us as we go through life. A child must learn to walk by himself, and in so doing must inevitably receive his share of bumps and bruises. As good parents we allow him the freedom to learn—even the freedom to fall and hurt himself. We do not will that he hurts himself but we allow him to accept the consequences of his mistakes. In the same way, God allows us to become sick or to suffer as the result of our own human frailties. He does not will us into our misery. The inference that a patient's plight is the will of God can have the effect of making his situation appear hopeless to him. If it's God's will, what's the use of trying? I'm afraid that that line of reasoning breeds a chain reaction of negativity in the patient and in those around him. I don't mean that we shouldn't face the facts and realize the possibilities for better or for worse, but we should leave the door open for healing even when hope is dim for the sick person's recovery.

"Leaving the door open" should not be a matter of

demanding more faith on the part of the sick person. Never should the patient be made to feel that it's all up to him, the opposite side of the coin from having it all left up to the will of God. He is doing his best, believing in the only way he is able. Just because we order it doesn't mean that he can come up with the kind of strong faith we may be wanting to see in him. In their own desperation for a healing miracle well-intentioned friends will say, "*if you only have faith enough,* you will be healed."

The kind of healing they are almost always referring to is the overcoming of the disease that afflicts the sick person. In the minds of most people healing automatically means healing of the body. Though a pastor's primary task with the sick is to heal, it is more important to heal the soul than the body. The person's salvation comes first. In the manual used by members of the Order of Saint Luke, a list of suggestions is given for planning a healing mission. When a healing mission comes to mind, again one thinks first of physical healings—the lame man throwing away his crutches, or the deaf man shouting with joy because he can hear again—yet, the directions in the manual point to the missioner's first duty:

> The object . . . is to save souls first and bodies second. To "save" them is to bring them to a state of Salvation (Latin: Salus, meaning health or wholeness). The Church's business is not merely to bring them into this state, but to keep them there.[3]

When we approach a seriously ill person, the most important healing to offer is the healing of the soul. That sometimes leads us to and involves us in an important pastoral responsibility to the sick: preparation for death. In the same way that some clergy are over cautious in their approach to spiritual healing, others are unwilling to consider the possibility that the sick person might die and should be prepared for death.

Emily Gardiner Neal[4] suggests that there must be different approaches to patients who are apparently dying. Although some can be given the facts, we know also that the truth might be too much for others to take. I personally feel that the true facts of the case should be shared whenever possible, because the human being has certain rights and responsibilities concerning death, particularly his own death. Too often in the effort to protect, loved ones deny the sick person those rights and opportunities.

"Don't worry about a thing—you'll be all better in no time."

"Of course you're not going to die—whatever gave you that crazy idea?"

"Death? Let's not talk about any such thing—you're doing fine."

These statements are typical of the stock answers commonly given by some who are seeking to protect their loved ones. The one who is dying often knows this and is often much better prepared to accept the truth than those who are trying to protect him. The family does a patient no good service if they have allowed him to die without an opportunity to put his house in order, without an opportunity to embrace a faith in God or to renew one that had become weak. He should also be given the satisfaction of giving directions concerning his burial, including requests for the clergyman, who will be handling the service.

Facing death is always a challenge. It is that inevitable trip which we all must make and to have it hanging heavily over one's head can be a fearsome thing. With no awareness of what is happening, with no planning and with no religious hope, meeting death can be a tragic experience for all concerned. However, with a healthy religious outlook and an understanding and acceptance of one's faith, death can be looked forward to as a great adventure. It is a pastoral duty of the Church to prepare people for that journey.

We pray for healing and we look for it with hope, but we

are mindful that the most complete healing, the only permanent healing, comes with the birth which we call death. No matter what gifts of healing we may have in the physical sense, this body is destined to wear out. So whether we die of sickness, accident, or old age, as Christians, we should learn to look at death without fear, for Christ has overcome death.

It is a privilege to minister to the sick who are healed in mind and spirit because they can be so casual about their illness and approaching death. The impact of their own spiritual healing is freely communicated to those around them, as they are made strong in their weakness. I had been called to the bedside of one of these, an old friend who had been lame during the latter part of her life, but who still gave out more good cheer than complaints. She knew that she was very weak, and as I prepared to leave she spoke.

"Whether I die or not matters little. I'm an old lady and I've had a good life. *I know* and *you know* where I'm going, so if my work is done here, then that's fine with me."

Two days later, while officiating at her funeral I felt no sense of grief. All I could feel was the joy of the Easter victory, "Because I live, you will live also" (John 14:19, R.S.V.). Her last words to me were words I could share with her friends on this day because they revealed her confidence in her Lord and her readiness to accept what was ahead. Through Christ she had overcome the fear of death.

My own wife's case was another example. Stricken with one of the most malignant and fastest growing types of cancer, she responded to it in a most unusual manner. When it was discovered under her arm and in her breast it had already spread too far to permit safe surgery, so radiation treatment alone was given. Of course, she regularly attended our healing service and had received the laying-on-of-hands and anointing. She was on many prayer lists near and far in this country and throughout the world. At first she had what appeared to be a complete remission for which we all rejoiced, but then the disease reappeared. At the end of three years from the beginning of her treatment she died—but what a glorious death!

Because of the extent of the cancer and the fact that it was a fast-growing strain, Joan was not given much hope for any kind of healing. Believing firmly in spiritual healing, we had no intention of giving up hope merely because of the grim diagnosis. The discovery of this disease is always a shock to those affected, and we were no exception to the rule. However, once we had accepted the facts as presented to us, we discussed our part in the experience. We decided that, no matter how the healing was to come—as immediate physical healing, as spiritual or mental healing, or as that perfect healing which comes with death itself—as Christians, we must use this illness as a means of witnessing in behalf of Christ and His Church.

I mentioned previously that there are cases where the sick person takes over the task of ministering to others instead of waiting to be ministered to by them. From the beginning of her illness Joan did that very thing—she ministered to others. As Sunshine Chairman of the women's group in our church she was not content merely to send a card or flowers, but personally visited the sick, even under the stress of pain and fatigue in herself. However, she did not convey that to the people she visited, for God always was there to supply the energy she needed for a given task. She continued this practice up until two or three weeks before her own death. God gave her the strength to remain active, keep cheerful and to be a constant witness to the availability of Christ in our lives today. Throughout the three year period she continued to sing in the church choir regularly, to take an elderly shut-in to lunch weekly, to maintain our household and entertain parishioners and friends—leading an active and useful life. Her doctor summed it up nicely.

"Joan, if I get sick I'm going to come and see you."

In *Where There's Smoke,* Mrs. Neal mentions what she

calls "redemptive suffering," a condition which I feel existed in Joan.

> If your healing is delayed you can be greatly blessed while you wait its completion, for illness can be an occasion for revealing God's glory and power in two ways: either by healing or by redemptive suffering, where pain is borne not in hopeless resignation, but offered as a willing sacrifice to God. I have found true redemptive suffering to be extremely rare; but I have witnessed it, and I have found it awe-inspiring.[5]

Two months before she died she felt that she had to write a letter to explain her feelings about her predicament to all her friends. After she completed the letter she asked me to read it, and then to put it away until after her death, when she wanted it sent to all. Because it conveys a feeling of confidence, faith, and a vital expectancy of the life that is to come, I want to share it with you as an example of one spiritually healed.

Dear Friends:
    As my days in this earthly kingdom are drawing to a close, and my entrance into Christ's heavenly kingdom approaches, His Holy Spirit compels me to write this letter to all of you.
    This is a time of great doubt and uncertainty—never before equaled in history. Man stands on the edge of the culmination of history. He can go on doubting and searching (God has given us the gift of choice—to accept or reject Him) or he can, by a willful act on his part, accept Christ as his Lord and Savior.
    Do you think that God created man just to have him destroy himself? He did not! God sent His only begotten son, Jesus Christ, into the world to show us how to live, how to die—and how to live again.
    We cannot save ourselves—but Christ can save us. Christ overcame death by his perfect obedience to and trust in God the Father. God must have known His son intimately to let Him come into the world. He knew it

was not going to be any "bed of roses" and surely it wasn't. It was for Him an uphill struggle all the way—but see where it ended—in victory over death.

And do you know that no one comes to the Father except by Christ Jesus? So it makes life so much more meaningful to us and to those with whom we come in contact if we become consecrated Christians while we are here.

Christ said, "I go to prepare a place for you. If it were not so I would have told you." *I believe in His word*—because what He says is God's word—*and what God promises He does.*

And now I'd like to say a few personal words to my dear friends. When it was confirmed three years ago that I had cancer and probably would have only a few months to live, this came as quite a blow to my husband, Mal, and me. We both prayed for the guidance of the Holy Spirit in our lives and for His supporting comfort. We asked, He gave, and we received in great abundance.

During the months of radiation treatments we were upheld by God's grace and by the loving prayers of countless friends such as you. These three years have been the most meaningful ones to me in my whole life—and I hope that this applies to others with whom I've shared Christ's life within my life. Now I know what St. Paul means when he says, "to live is Christ—to die is Christ."

There's such a thin veil, really, between this life and the life which is in heaven. In fact, we get glimpses of what the heavenly life is while we are right here on earth. Do not mourn my leaving—but rather rejoice with me that I go to see Him face to face . . . SEE YOU IN HEAVEN!

Much love in Christ,

Joan

Conscious up until the moment of death, she witnessed to the very end. Her mother and mine were tending to her needs and I was by the bedside, reading some selections from the

Book of Common Prayer. We all knew that the end was
near—we were just waiting. Just before it came she sat up in
bed, attentive as if listening. We asked if she needed anything
and she just shook her head. Then as we looked into her face
her eyes gazed in wonder high over our heads and her mouth
opened in awe—as one beholding some great and majestic
sight—and that was all. She never took another breath, nor
said another word, but we all got the message, and it was
good.

Earlier in my ministry I was called upon to pray for a
young woman from out of town who had been in a coma
following an accident and brain surgery. Naturally, in her
unconscious state, the patient did not know of my presence
there. Though I had been called upon to visit the patient, it
turned out that the people I talked with were the patient's
father and mother. How I wanted their daughter to respond
in some dramatic way to our prayers, to sit up in bed, all well
again. We continued to pray and wait, to pray and wait, all
through the night, and finally our waiting was over—she died.

I felt very bad for her parents and very inadequate as a
pastor. I had done all I knew. I had prayed with all the
sincerity and conviction I could muster and I had failed, or at
least I thought I had.

It wasn't until after the older couple had returned home
that I learned that God had allowed this experience to be a
spiritual awakening for them. Instead of feeling let down or
disillusioned by the apparent lack of response to our prayers,
they had been touched by the hand of God, which had
entered the sick room. I had been so intent in my
ministrations to the daughter that I had completely missed
seeing the change that took place in her parents.

Their own rector was the one who had seen the difference.
He had seen them before they left for the hospital, fearful,
apprehensive, and unsure of their own faith. Then he had
seen them again after their return, after he dropped by to
make arrangements for their daughter's funeral. He was

amazed at the difference. There was no need for him to offer comforting and consoling words, for again, *they* had become the ministers of God's word. They had come through this experience with a new awareness of God's love and a more mature understanding of the meaning of death to a Christian. After talking with them he was so impressed that he sat down right away and wrote me a letter to let me in on the good news.

"But not all are healed."

"True, if you insist on defining healing in the rather limited sense of a physical healing."

"But I'm afraid they might lose their faith if their loved one dies."

"What does Christ have to say on the subject?"

We continue to hear this dialogue from clergy and laity alike, because it is obvious to all who work with the sick that some patients do not get better. They don't all die from their illnesses, but many remain as chronic patients under treatment all through their lives. As a result, it is logical to ask questions concerning the Church's ministry of healing. I know this concern because I felt it so keenly myself at the beginning of my ministry. In my case, as I previously explained, I was catapulted from my cautious position right into the midst of healing activity. I was led from one situation to another which required my action in the form of healing ministrations. From my personal experiences in which the sick were healed it became very clear to me that prayer works and that miraculous cures are taking place all the time in our world today. Once I became convinced of this I did not feel I was doing my duty unless I were engaged in the healing ministry. I couldn't afford not to. I saw healing as something *I had to do* to be faithful to my calling.

"But, not all are healed?"

"Who are we to say?"

IV.
We Know So Little About It

The healing movement has spread through the Body of Christ wherever it is throughout the world. It has crossed denominational lines and has broken down the separation of clergy and laity through such organizations as the International Order of Saint Luke the Physician. Healing services are available in some form in almost every community in the nation. In spite of these things the average churchman is surprisingly ignorant concerning the healing activity in his church. Though prayer groups and their meeting times are listed in Sunday bulletins and healing services are scheduled, the average church member goes his own way in regard to these things. He's not too sure of what he thinks about his church's involvement in such matters, so he doesn't get involved.

In an age when our scientists are developing spacecraft and preparing for interplanetary travel it seems incongruous to some that we are using methods practiced by Jesus and the Apostles almost two thousand years ago. The antibiotics have been discovered and new surgical procedures such as open-heart surgery are being performed. We have "atomic cocktails," radiation therapy, and the use of the laser beam as a surgical instrument. We have new biologicals and pharmaceuticals every day and our research scientists tell of us even greater discoveries ahead.

Wade H. Boggs, Jr. has written a critical work on the healing movement[1] in which he brings up many questions people are asking, questions which should be satisfactorily answered. Don Gross takes a whole section in his book, *The Case for Spiritual Healing*[2], to deal with those questions and refute those statements in which Boggs challenges spiritual healing as it is being practiced today. The following statement is typical of Boggs:

> Ought not the Church perhaps to confine its interest to man's soul, to his character development, and leave the healing of the body to the medical profession?

Of course, the answer to this, from a medical, spiritual, or psychiatric viewpoint, is the fact that it is virtually impossible to deal with anything but the whole person. On the one hand, a person's attitude will affect the way in which he responds to a drug; on the other hand, a drug can change a person's attitude even when administered for a physical need. There is just no such thing as dealing with the physical body apart from the soul.

It is no wonder that some of us are hesitant about departing from accepted medical procedures when their only contact with spiritual healing is the one Oral Roberts show they saw on T.V. There is a common suspicion that spiritual healing is in opposition to science. Unfortunately, there have been "healers" who have encouraged people to ignore medical procedures and follow the spiritual approach exclusively. Also, there are established religious bodies such as the Christian Science church, who have traditionally discouraged healing through medical men. However, the great majority of those interested in spiritual therapy do not consider their work antagonistic to medical science. In fact, they consider themselves allies with doctors in the war against disease. In this vein Bernard Martin expresses the majority view:

Thus, while the Church must attempt to approach the problem of healing from a spiritual point of view, she should not, in any case, do so in opposition to medical science. Both ways are meant to meet, and when they do, the Church and medical science will become collaborators in a work which, under the guidance of the Holy Spirit, will seek only the true welfare of man.[3]

We must first realize that all healing comes from God, whether medicines or surgery are used, or prayer therapy alone, because we continually witness healing in both ways. We know that God can heal without the help of a medical man, but we also know that the greatest percentage of people are healed with the help of doctors and nurses. God always uses people to do His work, whether they are aware of it or not. As God uses men to baptize; to preach the good news; and to celebrate the Lord's Supper, He likewise uses men to do research; to immunize against polio, diphtheria, small pox, and other diseases; to perform surgery; and to use medicines (which He has provided) to combat disease. So, as Paul the Apostle worked side by side in a joint effort with Luke the Physician, we who represent the Church should be working in harmony with the forces of medical science. Let there be no question about it in the minds of both physicians anc clergymen—*we are on the same team.*

Once Christian people fully understand that they do not have to reject conventional medical treatment to accept a healing ministry, they have overcome one of the most significant barriers to active participation. The idea of a partnership is appealing to churchmen and medical men alike, as is evidenced by the large number of medical people who have become members of the order of Saint Luke. Because they are often placed on a pedestal it is easy to forget that doctors are people too—people who likewise need the support of our prayers. This was brought home to me as I visited a doctor who was hospitalized.

"I'd like to pray for you, Doctor, if you don't mind," I said with some hesitation.

"I'd like to have you do just that—and what do you mean, 'if I don't mind?' When you come to see me in the hospital, remember that I'm a member of your flock too, and I need your prayers just as much as anyone. We doctors are human too."

I left the room a bit chastened, but wiser, and through the years I haven't forgotten his advice. The same hesitancy I felt in myself I have observed in other members of the clergy in regard to doctors. Even in cases of spiritual healing it seems so important to us to obtain the endorsement of medical men. Certainly this is valid to a degree, for if there is to be a wedding of spiritual and medical forces, we should support one another. However, this should be a wedding in which the partners mutually respect the thinking and actions of one another.

After my ministry of healing in the Church had been extensive enough for me to relate experiences and compare them with others, I felt the need of discussing these things with my brother, who is a physician, and with other doctors as well. I wanted to know what medical men were thinking about the Church's ministry of healing; particularly, I wanted to know what they thought of my own part in it. I was really looking for their understanding, cooperation, and approval for my entering into "their field." I found out the doctors I knew didn't have any ready answer to explain away the results of spiritual healing and that their attitude was one of sympathetic interest (of course, there is a wide range of medical opinion about spiritual therapy, from outright hostility to the acceptance of some doctors who are doing spiritual healing as they practice medicine). I began to realize that doctors were as mystified by some of the responses to spiritual therapy as anyone else. Then it dawned on me that spiritual healing is "my field," properly in the realm of Church work. We have no right to be apologetic. We have been commissioned by none less than Jesus Christ himself to carry out a definite function. If that is the case, we should be the ones responsible for interpreting spiritual healing to the doctors, and not they to us.

If we are to work together as partners in a common cause it is necessary that those within the Church and those from the medical sciences understand each other. It is important for physicians to know what we are doing with their patients. Likewise, it is important for physicians to let us know what they are doing to our parishioners. One way for us to gain the proper respect of doctors and nurses is to learn proper behavior with the sick when they are hospitalized. There are rules and regulations concerning patients in hospitals and anyone who wants to help the sick should abide by those rules at all times. Unfortunately, some church callers, clergy and lay persons alike, have broken rules, overstayed their time, have used patients as captive audiences, have forced themselves on sick persons who did not wish to see them, have upset emotionally disturbed patients, and in general have made nuisances of themselves to the entire hospital staff. More than once have I been called upon to quiet patients who have been upset by such calls. In one case I was called in to comfort a young mother who had just lost a baby in child birth. She had been visited by an unauthorized preacher, whom she didn't know and didn't wish to see. He suggested to her that God had taken her child as a punishment for her evil ways. He was ejected from the hospital after the nurses heard the young woman's anguished cries for help. Another case was that of a woman recovering from major surgery, who had become emotionally upset following the visit of a young "progressive" minister, who insisted on arguing with her that there is no life after death. Naturally, in cases like these I also found it necessary to "unruffle the feathers" of the patients' doctors, and in one case, of the hospital administrator. I had to unruffle my own before I could even talk with them calmly.

We can never have complete control over those who may call in the Church's name, but we can do something about teaching good hospital manners within our associations and prayer groups. The more those engaged in spiritual healing can know of standard hospital practices and procedures, the more smoothly can they work side by side with medical personnel. As a seminarian I was made aware of the importance of knowing good sickroom manners and hospital procedures through my reading of the pioneer work by Richard C. Cabot and Russell L. Dicks, *The Art of Ministering to the Sick.*[4] Hospital Chaplain Russell Dicks, along with Dr. Cabot, a physician, collaborated in an effort to draw the physician's and clergyman's labors together in a common task. Dicks has continued to write in this general field and in *Pastoral Work and Personal Counseling* addresses the subject again:

> Marked gains have been made in bridging the gap between the physicians and clergymen; as we define our tasks more clearly and have a better understanding of each other's methods this gap will close more completely.[5]

In addition to knowing our way around the hospital and abiding by its rules, we can gain the confidence and cooperation of doctors by demonstrating to them our willingness to understand their work and problems. We can begin by learning something about the diseases they are combating as well as standard methods being employed in the treatment of disease. I stood in prayer by the side of a physician as he plunged a needle into the heart of a day-old child, administering adrenalin in a desperate move to give life to this infant; at that moment I felt nothing but profound appreciation for him and his profession. I likewise felt thankful that he had offered me the opportunity to share in his task. Such a shared ministry between doctor and pastor is good for all, the doctor, the pastor, and the patient. In one small town where I worked, the doctor, who had to make many house calls far into the night, used to ask me to ride with him at night to keep him company and to drive for him when he needed rest. I can remember a deep sense of sharing as I drove in the silence of the night with my physician-friend by my side, catching up on his sleep between house calls.

The better we know each other, the better we can work together. A physician is responsible for each patient under his care, under those circumstances he wants to be very sure of any person or persons who are attempting to apply any kind of additional therapy—spiritual or otherwise—to his patients. It is not unreasonable for him to want to know who we are and what we are doing as we call upon the sick. It is incumbent upon us to acquaint as many medical men as possible with the beliefs, hopes, and methods involved in spiritual therapy. A knowledgeable physician will call upon the services of the church, the same as any other member. One night around midnight I received a call from a young doctor in my parish.

"Father Miner, we've got a real sick baby out here—it's my own child and he's critically ill. I wonder if you could come out here to the hospital right away."

"Hang on, friend—I'll be right there."

As I entered the pediatric section I could sense the feeling of gloom and the futility as five doctors huddled silently in one corner of the room. One of them was the baby's father. When he saw me he jumped and led me by the arm to the incubator that held his tiny son, who was struggling for each breath.

"He's awful young, and awful sick, Father. We've done all we know, and it looks pretty bad—it's out of our hands now. Please, Father, do what you can."

I looked toward the corner of the room and noted the other doctors, sitting there like men dazed, motionless in their silence. This was a sick baby, but not only a sick baby.

It was *his baby*—their colleague and friend's own child. How they wanted to help! They had just functioned as a medical team, as they put into effect the best efforts of their combined skills; now I felt they were being called upon for another function, that of the prayer group. I didn't know what was going on in their minds, but if it wasn't prayer, then it was the closest thing they knew to prayer.

I washed my hands and put on a hospital gown, and inserting my arm through a small opening in the incubator, I placed my hand on the tiny form, offering him and his condition to God, asking for healing. After thanking God for hearing our prayers I went home again. Early the next morning I received a phone call. It was the baby's father.

"Chalk up another one for your side, Father, he's going to make it! He's made a wonderful recovery!"

"That's great news to hear but I'd call it more of a team effort."

"Yes, I know. But I also know how sick he was when I called you, and how dim our hopes were for his survival—so thank you!"

"And thank God, for He worked through all of us, I'm sure. I'm so happy for you and your family. Thanks so much for calling."

And that is the picture. God uses each one of us to perform His wonder. With a team concept we can do so much more in the war against disease. In the case above, God called upon the resources of medical science. They employed all the procedures they considered best for the infant's recovery, and used one of their tools, an incubator with oxygen, to ease the baby's breathing until yet another one of God's servants could arrive to perform his function in behalf of the sick child. Out of this team ministry came the gift of God's healing: a healthy, happy, baby boy.

I started this chapter by pointing out that many church people know little about spiritual healing as it is practiced today. Stranger still, many of the ordained clergy approach

spiritual healing with surprising caution. Some come to the
sickroom primarily to have a friendly visit and cheer the
patient, relegating prayer and other spiritual ministrations to
a secondary role or omitting them altogether. Others feel that
their main task as pastors is to comfort and console the sick
and help them to accept their suffering. There is a place for
both of these emphases, but when one refers to Holy
Scripture and our Lord's commission, there can be no
mistake as to what came first with Jesus: healing. His
command to us was *to go forth and heal.*

One reason that the general public knows so little about
healing in the Church is that so much of this ministry is done
in private, with individuals and small groups. Prayers are
offered in the home at the bedside of the sick person or in the
privacy of the hospital room. Doctors are rarely on hand to
witness such practices as the laying-on-of-hands or anointing
(Holy Unction), and even the nurses may be unaware of these
ministrations. The patient, himself, may be so sick that he
scarcely knows what is happening and, later on, may have
only a vague memory of the clergyman's visit. Daily,
countless numbers of sick people are receiving some kind of
spiritual therapy from ordained clergy, and also from lay
persons, who are active in the Church's healing ministry. In
spite of this, relatively few people are cognizant of all the
healing activity surrounding them.

Even in those churches where regular healing services are
publicly announced, only a small percentage of the total
congregation participates in those services. The Rev. Dr.
Alfred Price, internationally known for his work in spiritual
healing and as Warden of the Order of Saint Luke, told me
that his own eleven o'clock congregation on Sundays was
normal in this respect, that only a percentage of them were
actively involved in the healing ministry. It is those who have
need of healing in themselves or those who belong to the
prayer group who normally attend the week-day healing
services. It is significant, however, that more churches are

including one or more healing services as a part of their regular program. As that practice spreads more people in and out of the churches will have the opportunity to become better acquainted with the gift of healing through prayer, and the better acquainted people become with the ministry of healing, the more people will be healed.

V.
Healing is Loving

One thing is certain, while there are "differences of administrations" among those active in the healing movement, the common denominator which binds all together is love. See what some of the leaders in spiritual healing have to say.

Glen Clark: "The chief essential for spiritual healing the the capacity to love everything and fear nothing."[1]

John Ellis Large: "But many people—many more than we apparently seem sometimes to realize—must be loved back to health."[2]

Emily Gardiner Neal: "If one were searching for the single attribute most characteristic of the healing ministry, I suspect he would find that it is love."[3]

Agnes Sanford: "We are His channels for the sending out of His redemptive love into the world."[4]

Alfred W. Price: "We come today to receive Thy love, that Thy love may transform us and make us anew spiritually to receive Thy touch, to heal each one."[5]

As I related earlier in this book, I began a healing ministry with no special education on the subject. Full of doubts about spiritual healing, and unsure of my approach with the sick, nevertheless I did possess one necessary quality, the capacity to love. I think of how many times it is said of Jesus that "He had compassion" on those in need who were brought to Him.

Recalling the case of the first healing experience I

46

recognized as such—the complete healing of the woman in the coma—I remember that as her daughter approached me I had compassion on her. In spite of my uncertainty, in spite of my lack of knowledge concerning spiritual healing, I loved; through my love and the daughter's faith, the gift of health was received in the mother.

In the first letter of St. John we read, "Beloved, let us love one another: for love is of God; and everyone that loveth is born of God, and knoweth God" (I John 4:7). To that we might add that "everyone that loveth" can be used by Him in the healing ministry, for the power of God can overcome the deficiencies in man.

I recall an occasion where God used the love of an uninstructed child to manifest His glory. Our next-door neighbor was taken sick with a heart ailment, which gave her both pain and weakness. That was of deep concern to my seven year old twin daughters, who loved her dearly. Shortly after we had heard the sad news, the matter came up in the midst of our evening prayers. As we were going through our regular family prayers together one of my daughters burst out with a spontaneous prayer of her own.

"And please, God, make Mrs. R. all well again. Thank you, God."

We learned later that during that very night Mrs. R. had felt a profound change come over her, enough so that she had to come and tell us about it the next day. We told her of the spontaneous prayer offered by one and shared by all and she was thrilled to hear about it, on top of her experience of feeling "a newness" in her being. She continued to feel better; when she went to see her doctor he was most pleased with her progress and eventually released her with a clean bill of health.

My little girl's prayer was given in love and with thanks for the expected healing in her dear friend. That simple prayer had the ingredients for any healing prayer anywhere, for we pray lovingly—and we always give thanks. We thank God in the same breath that we pray for the sick person, knowing that He is already at work in us and through us to help the one in need, even before we finish our prayer.

The importance of thanksgiving in healing prayers was revealed to me when I began to make thanks a regular part of my prayers for the sick. The "thank you" as a part of the request for healing made everything complete. I could see that it gave confidence and expectancy to the one for whom we were praying, as well as to the one who was offering the prayer. That point was first brought home to me as I read Agnes Sanford's *Healing Light,* but it did not have any real impact on me until I began to adopt it as *my own practice.* Now, if at the end of a prayer request we say, "Thank you God," does that mean that we shouldn't ask for healing in that person again? I don't think so.

I've often been asked this, and also the matter of repeating the laying-on-of-hands for healing in people, particularly those who appear to have a chronic type of illness. As far as God is concerned we need to ask only once. The minute we turn over a problem to God it is in His hands and He will act on it. However, as imperfect creatures, we are most often in need of reassurance, and it helps to receive these "outward and visible signs" of what is already going on within us. Mrs. Sanford expresses this quite nicely, I feel:

> Most of us need every day to enter into God's presence and focus out attention first upon Him and then upon the area that needs healing, so that God may have every opportunity of continuing His creative work in us. But after the first time, we may say, "thank you" instead of "please."[6]

So after we say "please" once, it really doesn't matter how many times we repeat our thanksgivings. As I said above, the ingredients for any healing prayer must always involve love and thanksgiving. Each compliments the other. Later on I shall say something about the need for a group of concerned persons to be associated with a healing ministry, a group which does just this: offers prayers in love and publicly expresses thanks to God for His "inestimable love" for answering those prayers. John Ellis Large refers to such a group, whether it be a prayer group, study group, or worship fellowship, as "the loving congregation," not just the congregation, but always the *loving* congregation.[7]

Jesus commands us to "love one another" as He has loved us. Whenever people really take Him seriously on this subject, the healing power is released, whether in a case of organic disease or in human relations. We are "made perfect in love," we cast out fear through love, and by the power of love we can knock down the fences that separate nation from nation, race from race and man from man.

Once I went to work in a new environment, where the job was different for me, and where all the people strangers to me. The person I was to be in closest contact with in this work was a Negro. I suppose that, on the day I first met him, the thing that made him seem different from the others was his color, for he was the only Negro employed there at that time. Days, weeks and months passed as we worked together, conversing, sharing—really getting to know one another—and the longer I worked with him, the less conscious I was of a racial difference. Because I was new to the job, he helped me learn the procedures; it was he who introduced me to the other workers. We became close friends and in our friendship was a mutual trust and respect that might otherwise be described as love. Eventually I was no longer aware of his color nor he of mine. We could only see each other as friends—as brrothers.

If we human beings could only dare to trust God and deal with our fellow men of all races and nationalities in love, we could wipe out the diseases that infect us as we relate to other human beings. We are afraid to put our trust in God and "go out on a limb," making the first move in love as we deal with those of different races, creeds, and nationalities.

As sinful men, we let pride make us wait for each other; neither party wants to risk making the first loving gesture in such relationships as a troubled marriage, a rift between labor and management, a problem between the races, or a dispute between nations. "Saving face" continues to be so important, even if it means death and destruction for the ones who are involved. On the other hand, the admission of guilt seems every bit as difficult for a group or a nation as it is for the lone penitent at the altar rail. But the way of love is God's way, and God's way is the only way to wholeness and health.

We know that love is a healing force combating all forms of illness. One form of illness which has plagued mankind is alcoholism. While we know of many cases of spiritual healing in alcoholics, we also realize that countless others have been assisted by AA, psychologists, psychiatrists, social workers, and physicians who make a specialty of treating that sickness. Again, regardless of who is working with the alcoholic, love is an important factor in successful therapy. Likewise, the absence of love in a person, particularly in his formative years, is seen as a causative factor in mental and emotional problems and in alcoholism. In his book on counseling with alcoholics, Howard J. Clinebell, Jr., points a finger at the church, suggesting that the local congregation has not always been a receptive and loving group to those in need.

> If the church had more often offered a fellowship that was "healthy and pleasant and warm" to children and youth and parents and families, it might have done more than it has toward preventing emotional ills, as well as making it unnecessary for persons to find their fellowship in taverns.[8]

I'm afraid that this situation is sometimes true even when we are trying to be a friendly group. In Alaska we observe that while many of the Indian and Eskimo people from the "Bush" are unable to identify with the city church, with its many middle-class overtones, they are often very much at home in the local bars, where they find easy acceptance with the bartenders and clientele. The church people want to be friendly, but their fine clothes, educated talk, and different social behavior make them seem unapproachable. In the bar it is different. The uninhibited group there appears to be more genuine to them. Of course, we can't lay all the blame on circumstances beyond our control. We must admit that sometimes we who are within the church are not "the loving congregation" that we're supposed to be.

Still speaking on the subject of love, Clinebell calls it a preventive medicine for alcoholism and other ills, and makes some concrete suggestions to the Church for teaching the parents of young children.

> Through such a program parents could come to see that healthy personality is "home made" and that an ounce of mother is worth a pound of psychiatrist. Such parent education should put particular emphasis on helping the parents of infants to satisfy their babies' oral needs, the babies being allowed abundant sucking and given cuddling as well of generous amounts of "t.l.c." [tender loving care]. By helping parents to do that which they basically want to do but often cannot-namely, raise children who are mentally, emotionally, and spiritually healthy—the church would help to prevent alcoholism at its very roots.[9]

This advice would not only help to prevent alcoholism, but would help children grow into the healthy beings God desires them to be. For the child who is loved becomes a loving person, with the capacity for health in himself and for healing in others, for healing is loving.

Read Jesus' own words on the subject of love:

> I have loved you just as the father has loved me. You must go on living in my love. If you keep my

commandments you will live in my love just as I have
kept my Father's commandments and live in his love. I
have told you this so that you can share my joy, and
that your happiness may be complete. This is my
commandment: that you love one another as I have
loved you (John 15:9-12, Phillips).

VI.
Healing is Forgiving

"The Church's Ministry of Healing" comprehends those methods employed by the Church Universal in all its branches which have been handed down from the earliest days ... The healing methods most commonly used have been three: (a) The Ministry of Confession and Absolution; (b) The Laying-on of Hands with Prayer; and (c) Anointing with consecrated Oil, administered with Prayer as taught by St. James[1]

In this chapter I propose to deal with the first of these three, "The Ministry of Confession and Absolution" otherwise described as the Sacrament of Penance or Forgiveness. In non-Catholic circles all you have to do to "get a rise out of" a group is to mention the Catholic practice of confession. Quickly, different individuals will take the floor to state their opinions on this subject.

"No priest has the power to forgive sins—only God can do that."

"I know plenty of Catholics who make their confession on Saturday nights and then go out and commit the same sins all over again."

"All you need is a penitent heart and God will forgive your sins if you just pray to Him alone."

All of these statements are true as far as they go, but they don't go far enough. For instance, while it is true that on his own authority no man, priest or otherwise, can forgive sins (nor, for that matter, heal), in the name of Jesus Christ he

53

may pronounce God's forgiveness, or baptize, or lay hands upon the sick, or anoint with oil. When men are ordained from the ministry of the Church they are set apart and commissioned to act in behalf of their Lord. It was Christ's own idea to ordain His disciples and to give them authority to act in His name. That means that in any confession where an absolution is given, the Minister (and that includes the Roman Catholic priest) is carrying out the orders from on high; he is acting in Jesus' name (see John 20:23).

Concerning the statement that Catholics confess their sins, then go out and sin again, don't we all? Those sins which tend to beset us the most are the sins that we find easiest to repeat. The same sins return to plague us, whether we are pillars of the church or no. The men who were about to stone to death a woman found in adultery were members in good standing in their community and congregation. Yet, when Jesus stopped them and said, "He that is without sin among you let him first cast a stone," no one could do it. In the entire Church throughout the world, all of the members are urged to sin no more, but sin still continues to be the primary cause of man's misery.

The third statement is also true, that God will forgive your sins as you come to Him in the privacy of your home with a penitent spirit. But the fact remains that that does not seem to be sufficient for many. The feeling of guilt continues to appear as the cause of illness in people, even Christian people who have poured out their hearts to God in prayer. The heavy weight of a sin kept to oneself was recognized even in New Testament times as St. James urged the faithful to "confess, therefore, your sins one to another . . . that ye may be healed" (James 5:16).

The importance of confession is seen by one of today's outstanding authorities in the field of pastoral psychology, Dr. Leslie D. Weatherhead, who writes about it in *Prescription for Anxiety.*

One objection will quickly leap to the mind, "Is it not sufficient to confess to God?" to which the answer clearly seems to be, "Yes, quite sufficient, as long as God is real," but so many people complain, in regard to their prayers, that they feel as though they are talking to nothing. If that is true, then the prayer of confession will not have enough feeling about it to make it cathartic. The man who prays will feel frustrated. It is a poor game trying to feel forgiven.[2]

As a parish priest of the Episcopal Church I have received personal testimony from many persons on the difficulty people have in feeling forgiven about something they have been keeping to themselves. The amazing thing to know is that the sin need not be very significant, from a general viewpoint, to cause great trouble. It is how large the sin appears to be to the one feeling guilt that is important. Often these sins have been carried with the individual for years, and with the passage of time they have been magnified many times.

"Oh if I'd only known about making a confession before in our church. I've been a Churchman all my life and I've been miserable with this feeling of guilt for over ten years. No one ever told me that I could make a confession in our church and now that I've done this I feel wonderful, like a new person. Thank you for telling me about the sacrament of Forgiveness."

Here was a case of an active Christian mother and wife, haunted by a sin which loomed large in her conscience for over ten years—a sin she was unable to share first with her parents, then with her husband—though she continually acknowledged her penitence to God in private. You might conjecture that if this were the case, God forgave her sin years ago, the first time she made her confession to Him in private, and you would be right. The only problem was that she didn't know it, or feel it, or recognize it. Though God forgave her, she couldn't forgive herself.

Another thing to know about the healing which comes from forgiveness is its suddenness and completeness. In the course of counseling with the lady mentioned above, she had mentioned being troubled by a feeling of guilt. However, she did not want to tell me about it in my office—it seemed too embarrassing that way. I suggested to her that she could confess this impersonally in the church, not to me as counselor and friend, but to her pastor as Christ's representative. I made an appointment with her for another tme, so that she could adequately prepare herself. When she kept that appointment she went directly to the church, to the altar rail and knelt down near a priest in vestments and stole; in his presence she could confess her sin to God. There was no conversation such as "How do you do" or "It's good to see you," but merely the carrying out of a task. Finally, after receiving a brief counsel and directions for making an act of thanksgiving (penance), she heard Christ's appointed representative pronounce forgiveness in the Master's name. Then she heard him say the following words.

"Go in peace. The Lord hath put away all thy sins."

But she couldn't go. She was bent over the altar rail, sobbing—sobbing tears of cleansing, tears of relief, tears of joy. It took only a few minutes of her time, but in those few minutes she received a new lease on life and a greater realization of God's love and forgiveness. The big hurt that had been with her so long had disappeared and in its place was the great joy of one who has been "born again."

The fact that the confessional can be abused should not blind us to the realization that it is an effective channel of God's grace to man. Not always is the sacramental confession in the church necessary—but the principle that man's deep guilt feelings should be released in the presence of another person is used not only by clergymen, but also by psychologists and psychiatrists. Within the successful program of Alcoholics Anonymous, this advice is found in the famous "twelve-step" plan of rehabilitation. Step Four involves making "a searching and fearless moral inventory" of one's life. This is followed by Step Five, which is essentially the making of a confession: "Admitted to God, to ourselves, and to another human being the exact nature of our wrongs."

The reaction of the person described above, who was healed through forgiveness, is quite typical of experiences I have shared as both priest and penitent. There is often this overflow of tears, tears which literally wash away all feelings of guilt and make one clean again. Also typical are the expressions of joy, as well as of chagrin about not having heard sooner of the availability of confession apart from Roman Catholic usage.

One Sunday, following the church service, a stranger approached me with a sense of urgency as I shook hands with the people filing out the front door. I could hear the note of desperation in his voice and could see the pain in his face, so I excused myself from the people and took him aside.

"Reverend—Father—or whatever they call you—I'm not a member of your church. You see, I was brought up a Methodist. Well, someone told me I could make a confession in your church. I'm not a Catholic, but I'm going to go crazy if I don't get this thing off my chest. It's ruining my marriage, my work, I can't eat or sleep. Oh please help me—I can't stand it any more."

This was a matter for immediate attention, and yet there were people everywhere—in the church, in the parish halls, milling around the grounds. I took him into one of the church school rooms and told him to let it all out—anyway as much as he wanted to—and he did. It was as though the dam had burst as his pent-up accusations of guilt poured forth, ridding him of their poison. When he finished I explained to him that God required only this: to honestly admit our wrong doings, to say that we're sorry, and to propose to do better in the future. I told him that when we had fulfilled those conditions, His forgiveness followed. I gave him a brief word of counsel and then pronounced the absolution according to the practice of our church. Following that act I witnessed a spiritual healing in this man.

He had knelt before me as a figure of despair, a broken spirit in a body crumpled in an attitude of complete unworthiness. As I concluded the prayer of absolution he remained there motionless. Then, before my eyes it seemed as though I could see strength being poured into him. When he finally stood up I looked into his face and saw a different person from the one who had approached me just a few minutes before. This one seemed at least a foot taller, full of joy and new energy. This one was cleansed, like Isaiah—and like Isaiah, who said, "here am I, send me," this new man wanted to live for God as a servant in His Church.

I saw him months later at a church conference, but didn't know who he was. He made himself known to me and told me that his confession had truly been the beginning of a new life for him and his family. In the time that had passed he had identified with a church near his home and, with his family, had become seriously involved in the life of the congregation.

He continued to be strong in his life, in his marriage, in his work, and in his faith. The reason he was at the conference was that he had been chosen as the official lay delegate from his parish. He was truly a different man from the one who had first tugged at my arm in desperation.

The reason for my dwelling on this subject is the fact that the tendency to hide one's own guilt is so universal. Take any group of children throwing stones: a window is broken and the first thing you hear is, "He did it," before the question is even asked. My wife used to chide me whenever we heard on a favorite recording Adam's answer to God in the Garden of Eden, "That woman whom thou gavest to be with me, *she* gave me of the tree, and I did eat." Joan used to say, "Adam was a typical man—passing the buck to his wife."

And it is true that ever since the dawn of civilization man

has been passing the buck to the nearest scapegoat he can find. The sad part is that it applies not only to individuals, but likewise to groups. Hitler and the Nazis blamed the Jews for Germany's problems. The Negros blame the Whites for social problems, and the Whites react by blaming the Negro demonstrations for all the trouble. If you happen to be a Republican, you know that the Democrats are to blame, and so forth, long into the night. On the national and world scene even nations follow this practice, presenting themselves blameless in any controversy. It is always "the other guy." But if we have a sickness within ourselves which we refuse to recognize, there is no way to bring about a cure. As Jesus plainly said, "You hypocrite, first take the log out of your own eye, and then you will see clearly to take the speck out of your brother's eye" (Matthew 7:5 R.S.V.).

The importance of self-examination, where we own up to our own mistakes, confessing them to God and disposing of them, cannot be overemphasized. If we wish to go forth to heal the sick we must be sure that we are cleansed of all bitterness, envyings, hostilities, and prejudices, so that we can freely demonstrate the love of God in our lives. Jesus came into the world and gave His life for the forgiveness of sins. One of the great tragedies in the history of mankind is that so many have not availed themselves of this forgiving and healing grace. Would that we could start each day with penitent hearts and a grateful acknowledgment of his forgiveness in our lives.

We know that a feeling of guilt is common among those with mental and emotional illnesses. Psychiatrists regularly use "cartharsis," which is the elimination of one's fears and anxieties through talking them out with the doctor. When a patient has guilt feelings he is encouraged to get them out into the open, where they may be examined in the light and rendered helpless. If more people in the church were to avail themselves of the healing of confession and absolution, fewer cases of mental and emotional illness would result.

I had a rather unusual experience with a woman who was obviously mentally disturbed—so much so that I seriously considered calling a psychiatrist in immediately. I have been involved with the mentally ill enough to recognize signs of this illness in people. The woman who appeared at my office door had all these signs. Her husband, who had brought her to me, had very little control over anything she did. She was wild-eyed, incoherent in her speech and appeared highly agitated in her behavior. As a matter of fact, I was not very happy to have the husband close the door and leave me alone with her. Nevertheless he did just that.

She sat down and started what seemed a never-ending stream of words and phrases from which I was able to determine two things. First, she got the point across to me that she and her husband had driven over two hundred miles to see me. Second, the main thing that was troubling her was a feeling of guilt, which she said was "unbearable." I managed to break into her conversation and tell her of the forgiveness of sins, and that was exactly what she had been waiting for. That was why she practically forced her husband to get in their truck and drive over two hundred miles on icy roads in the dead of an Alaskan winter. Again it was a familiar pattern: sins which had accumulated for years gushed out uncontrollably. Finally she stopped talking.

I gave her the assurance of God's pardon right there in my office. I was not prepared for her reaction. As I gave her the absolution and informed her that "God had put away" all her sins, a calm came over her and she seemed to go limp in the chair. It startled me a bit, but then I noticed that the wildness had gone out of her eyes and that she was no longer agitated. Then she smiled at me. When she spoke it was in clear coherent speech, in complete contrast to her previous behavior. I called for her husband, and you never saw a more surprised man in your life. They looked at each other, they embraced, and they walked off arm in arm, happy to have found each other again. And all I could think was "Thanks be to God for his unspeakable gifts."

I had learned previously that healing is *loving.* Now I knew beyond a shadow of a doubt that healing is *forgiving.*

VII.
Mental and Emotional Illness

A person's spiritual problems can never really be isolated from other parts of his nature. The spiritual, mental and emotional aspects are intertwined with each other and with the physical condition as well. Certainly, we could call the cases cited in the preceding chapter valid examples of therapy with mental and emotional problems, even though all of them involved feelings of guilt and matters of conscience and moral judgment. One of the major concerns of the day is a social illness, the sick marriage. Counselors in and out of the Church are coming to recognize that marriages are susceptible to illness and death, as is borne out by the alarming divorce rate in our country today. A physician, Dr. William L. Carrington, has written about unhealthy marriage in his book, *The Healing of Marriage.*

Marriages like people, can sicken and die. The sickness of marriage may be acute or chronic, mild or severe, general or limited to one aspect of the relationship, one part of the "body". It may be progressive or recurrent, obvious or hidden, comparable in all these respects with the sickness of persons . . . Sick and broken marriages, like sick and broken persons, can be healed.[1]

Most healing of marriages is carried on by marriage counselors, social workers, physicians, psychologists, psychiatrists, and clergymen in the form of counseling. No longer is counseling a matter of a "between the halves" pep talk in which the couple is told to shape up and get on with the job. Neither is it just a matter of trying harder or listening to words of advice from the counselor. It is usually a lengthy and difficult task in which the man and wife are guided by the counselor as they work out their own diagnoses and solutions to their problems. There is usually no short-cut. The marriage takes a long time to get into a mess so it is reasonable to expect to take considerable time and effort to root out the causes of illness.

Whether he likes it or not the average clergyman will become involved with sick marriages. I have always been glad that my undergraduate work was in the field of psychology and that I did some graduate study in counseling. At least when I began counseling people I had received instruction in the basic professional procedures. Through the active work of counseling and continued reading on the subject I became more proficient with the passage of time. You may be wondering why I have gone off on this tangent with this discussion of marriage counseling in a book on spiritual healing. You must remember that every marriage is made up of two individuals whose personal health of mind, body, and soul has a direct relationship with the health of their marriage. Spiritual healing in the husband and wife becomes a like cure in the marriage.

There are many handicaps that face the clergyman as he attempts to function as a counselor. Some have little or no training in the field. Most others lack adequate staff and facilities for counseling on a large scale. There is one advantage the clergyman counselor has over the others, where the marriage problems are of a religious or moral nature. Here, confession, with its healing absolution, can be especially useful. Here too, the laying-on-of-hands with prayer may not only heal wounds, but also offer a continual guidance through a closer relationship with God. The pastor also has the authority to teach and explain how Christian beliefs, when applied to the home, become Christian living, and how that results in a happy marriage, a marriage where their *praying together* keeps them *staying together.*

In cases of Christian healing, God often requires much work from us in effecting a final cure. As I mentioned above, marriage counseling often goes on over a long period of time. Sometimes our prayers act as catalysts to continued probing and discussion between the husband and wife. By beginning with God and listening to his direction they can forge ahead, aware of their difficulties but confident of a final solution to their problem. They can persevere because they know that "If God be for us, who can be against us?" (Romans 8:31 K.J.V.) is a reality they can count on to see them through.

Though we tend to think of healing in respect to bodily ailments the influence of God's healing power is constantly being experienced over a wide range of personal and group ailments. Emily Gardiner Neal refers to a variety of other than bodily sicknesses healed in just one mission.

> The healing ministry is not limited to the physicially sick. At that same altar rail, before the night was over, occurred other healings which equaled and perhaps surpassed in wonder those I have just described.
> There was the healing, for example of almost unendurable grief, suffered by a couple whose five children had been burned to death the month before; there was the instantaneous healing of an alcoholic, who from that day to this has never desired a drink, and there was a reconciliation between father and son, separated for ten years until that night. In healings like these, we watch with awe-struck eyes the work of the Holy Spirit, as, strengthening, healing, and sanctifying, He guides us into all truth.[2]

Among the healings she relates there is one of an alcoholic who was instantaneously healed. In regard to the healing of marriages I mentioned the laying-on-of-hands acting as a catalyst to further action. That is sometimes the case with healing in alcoholics. On a dark and dreary Ash Wednesday in Alaska a drunken man came stumbling into my office late in the afternoon. His body reeked of alcohol and he looked more savage than man, his heavy growth of beard giving him a general appearance of dishevelment. Though his words were slurred, his mind was surprisingly keen as he explained to me the purpose of his visit.

"You may not believe it but I know this is Ash Wednesday and I haven't been to church for months. Would you believe I used to have a nice wife and a darling daughter? No more, they're gone now and it's my own damned fault. I'm a drunk, and I don't blame them for leaving me. Father, I believe in God. I know this is Ash Wednesday and I should have been to receive communion and ashes this morning but I didn't make it. Can you do something for me, Father? I don't have the guts to quit and I know it's killing me."

"Have you tried AA?" I asked.

"Talk, talk, talk, that's all they want to do. Will ya help me, Father?"

I can give you the laying-on-of-hands and offer a prayer for you. Do you feel guilty about your drinking? Are you sorry about it and do you wish to acknowledge this to God?"

"I sure do, Father, and Father, I want you to pray for me—I've had it."

I asked him to follow me into the church. We knelt down together at the altar rail and the first thing I did was to help him to get rid of his guilt feelings through acknowledging his repentance to his God. That he did gladly and without hesitation, which enabled me to use the absolution and assure him of God's forgiveness. I followed with the laying-on-of-hands and a prayer for guidance in his life. He thanked me and without ever giving me his name he disappeared out the front door of the church.

About a month later a newcomer came to the services one Sunday morning. He was a good looking, clean-cut type of business man, who mentioned that he had recently begun work in our community. He rather surprised me when he said that he knew me, even though I did not know him. He continued to come to the church services on a regular basis, and finally explained his curious statement.

"I know you've been thinking that you met me before. I can see you're trying to figure out where you met me. Well, I've kept you in the dark long enough. I'm the drunk who came to see you on Ash Wednesday!"

He explained that following our shared experience in the church he had gone to his rooming house and fallen into a deep sleep for hours. When he awoke he had something to eat, then cleaned himself, and went out to make a phone call. It was to the AA number listed in the paper. Immediately he became active in the AA program, and by the time he came to services that first Sunday he had found good employment. This healing was not instantaneous, like the one described above by Mrs. Neal. He had to work hard, following the Alcoholics Anonymous program suggestions. He put his heart and soul to this task and eventually became one of the outstanding leaders for AA in our area. He was my chief contact on alcoholic problems and he rendered me invaluable assistance in explaining alcoholism and the AA program to others in need. In this case the healing literally directed his life into new channels and widening opportunities to serve God and his fellow man.

Another incident involving drinking, but not alcoholism, was the time the police called me to help them subdue one of my parishioners who had gone on a rampage in a local bar. The police knew him as ordinarily a law-abiding citizen, and wanted to avoid using strong-arm tactics to bring him under control. I wasn't enthusiastic about going into the bar for him. It seemed just a little bit like Daniel going into the lion's den, and I didn't feel as secure as Daniel is reported to have been. The man out of control was a big person and he had intimidated everyone in the bar, so like Dopey in *Snow White and the Seven Dwarfs,* I was sort of pushed into the bar with the others right behind me—way behind me.

I really felt relieved when he reacted like a small boy being caught stealing the jam, as soon as he recognized my clerical collar. Just as peaceful as a lamb he walked with me to the police car and got in without an argument. Once under way he started to get unruly again, but all I had to do was to speak his name and he'd say, "Sorry, Father," and calm down. Because he had caused some damage the police felt they should keep him overnight, so they put him in a cell. As soon as they closed the door on him he began to scream in genuine terror, complaining that "they were after him all over the place." Later on I learned that he was reliving an experience from the war where he had been trapped in a shell-hole with two Japanese soldiers, both of whom he had to kill.

"Let me out of here—they're gonna get me. Oh my God, let me out of here!"

I could see that this wasn't any ordinary case of drunkedness, but something deeper and much more complex. This was a sick man, there was no doubt about that. I managed to get his attention, and again, when he saw me he was able to concentrate on what I was saying, even though he was still cringing against the wall. He was panting and the beads of perspiration covered his brow. It was a pitiful sight to behold. He spoke to me.

"Doesn't anyone understand?"

"Yes, there is Someone who understands. Jesus understands."

"Can He help any—can He do anything?"

"Yes, through me He can give you His blessing."

"Will it help?"

"Yes, I'm sure it will help."

I made the sign of the cross toward him and gave him the blessing "in the name of the Father and of the Son and of the

Holy Ghost." Then a most remarkable thing occurred. Standing against the wall he looked like he'd been shot. With a dazed look on his face his body went limp and he slid down the wall on to the bed and rolled over sound asleep. One of the policemen stood there with his mouth agape, completely dumbfounded.

"I never saw anything like this in my life before!"

Though I felt the same as he did, I never let on that this wasn't normal procedure in my book. Before leaving the station I told the officer that I felt that the man was sick and should be in a hospital rather than a jail cell. The following day he was taken to a V.A. hospital where he was treated, responding well to psychotherapy. Later on I learned from one of the doctors that he had told them the only one who believed he was sick was the young priest, and he appreciated that. This is not an example of a complete healing, but it was spiritual therapy, and it gave him all the relaxation and sleep that he would have received from sedation in the hospital.

An example of spiritual healing in one with emotional problems was the case of a man in his early forties who was brought to our healing service. All I knew about him was the fact that he had problems. As I gave him the laying-on-of-hands I could see a profound reaction in that his whole body trembled violently as I touched him with my hands. He was visibly moved by that experience and following the service we had a talk together. There was an obvious rapport between us and I imagined that this might be the beginning of a lasting friendship. Before he was able to come to another of my healing services he was dead. Shocked as I was to learn of his death, I was overjoyed to learn that the result of his visit to the church was a complete restoration of his faith, a new and courageous outlook on life, and a renewed spirit that showed forth to all who were close to him. He died, but he died happy to go forward to meet a Lord with whom he had just been reunited. And though our meeting together was brief, I still believe that it was the beginning of a beautiful friendship which we shall renew.

The varieties of healings and the ways in which they are brought about are without number. One of the common ailments of our time is fatigue. The advertisements ask you if you have "tired blood" or a vitamin shortage, and after a session as Den Mother for a gang of Cub Scouts you feel like you have both. It was during such a low as this that I tried a kind of prayer therapy for my wife, who had been pushing all day and still had a busy evening schedule ahead. When I left her she was completely exhausted, flopped in a chair, as I called out to her that I'd pick her up in a half-hour.

Alone in my car I realized how tired she seemed to be, so I pulled over to the side of the road so that I could concentrate on a prayer. I thought of her in her exhausted condition and then of her in a rested and refreshed condition. I prayed that a new surge of energy would sweep over her so that she could meet the obligations of the evening ahead.

As I walked into the house thirty minutes later I was greeted by my wife's cheery voice and she looked just great.

"Right after you left I was still relaxing in the chair when I felt a new surge of energy (my very words) come over me. I got up feeling full of pep and I still do. You prayed for me, didn't you?" I nodded "yes" but even so, I was surprised at the change in her.

All of us should be more alert to make use of such prayers as this daily. Seeing others in their best light, as God would have them be, we help to remove them from mental depression and emotional exhaustion. This is also an effective way of praying for someone who is giving us a hard time, a supervisor or fellow worker. We just surround him with the love of God and pray for him, thinking of how God sees him with His all-surpassing love. And after a while that person begins to look a little better to us, too.

We need no theological degrees or holy orders to pray for others. The ministry of healing is not restricted to the clergy;

from earliest times it has been shared by the priesthood of all believers." Once baptized into the Body of Christ we all become grafted to that Body as participating parts. The divine commission is meant for all who owe allegiance to Christ as Savior and Lord, and a part of that commission is to go and heal. The average person might feel a little strange laying hands upon the sick, but certainly should not feel any qualms about offering special intentions for those known to be in need of health, mental, emotional or physical. This is a labor of love that we all can do.

VIII.
God's Anesthesia

In the preceding chapter I compared the therapy with the distraught man in the jail cell to that of a sedative administered in the hospital. Sedatives are given to relieve pain, to relax a patient and to allow someone who is suffering to sleep. All kinds of anesthesia come from God, in that He placed the ingredients for them upon this earth and then gave man the intelligence to know how to use them. In my personal experience in the healing ministry I have often been permitted to be a channel for the giving of God's anesthesia through prayer and the laying-on-of-hands.

My physician-brother's specialty is anesthesiology. He administers the anesthetic to the patient undergoing surgery, rendering the person insensible to pain. In the practice of general medicine there are numerous other pain relievers regularly used to help people tolerate suffering. By and large the greatest number of people suffering from pain are relieved by these means.

My first experience with God's anesthesia came out of an urgent need. I was called to the bedside of a man dying from heart disease. He was in great pain, but because he disagreed with the use of barbiturates there was nothing his doctor could do for him. Being a deeply religious man he asked them to send for his pastor. It was about 11:30 P.M. on Easter Even when I arrived at the bed of my dying friend. He was suffering intensely and his breathing was labored. He managed a half-smile when he recognized me.

71

"Hello Pastor, glad to see you. Looks like I'm going home and I'm glad, but I am hurting pretty bad, having a hard time breathing. I won't take that dope they're trying to give me, so maybe if you pray for me that'll help."

This conversation took about all the strength he could muster so I asked him no more, except to point to where the pain was the greatest. Once I had determined the area of pain, which was his chest, I placed my hands there and prayed. As I mentioned before, he breathing was convulsive and my hands moved up and down as he struggled for each breath. And then relaxation took over and he began to breathe easily. He stopped his moaning and went into a gentle sleep. Though he lasted through the night until sunrise on Easter morning his breathing never became labored again nor did he feel pain again. God's anesthesia had lulled him to sleep until he could wake to celebrate Easter on the other side.

You might ask if that was just the power of suggestion? I must respond that I do not know how much the power of suggestion enters into it. What I do know is that a man who was suffering greatly was greatly relieved. It is not unreasonable to assume that God, who supplied our systems with antibodies to ward off disease, would not also give us psychic powers which would enable us to combat pain. In this whole field of spiritual healing much is still unknown about the exact manner in which people are healed. Medical research people may some day define and catalogue different kinds of spiritual healing as more is learned about it, but that is not the job of the Church. Our job is still to follow orders. As we go about the task of bringing health to the sick we are to use those means at our disposal, those methods which have been passed down through the ages from Christ Himself. And those methods still work.

I was called to the house of a good friend who was in excruciating pain, so severe that he couldn't sit down or lie down in any position. They had called the doctor, but the prescription for pain didn't touch it. Not knowing where else to turn they called me, asking if I would come by and see what prayer would do.

When I arrived he was in a constant state of motion, so I asked him if he could just stop long enough for me to administer the laying-on-of-hands. He sat down on a chair in front of me and I put my hands on the affected spot, his hip. As my hands rested on that part of his body he spoke òf receiving the sensation of heat.

"It feels warmer than a hot water bottle—it's a real deep heat."

Before he could say any more he was in a sound sleep. I looked at his wife and put my hands in hers so she could feel their temperature.

"You see, my hands are not even very warm. What he felt was the sensation of God's own heat which was flowing through my body."

He didn't move again while I was there. He didn't hear me leave, but continued to sleep for hours. Again, additional medical treatment was required before his problem was taken care of through surgery. But for the time being he was relieved of the pain. As the little girl said, he had received one of those "shots" which we more commonly call the laying-on-of-hands with prayer, and it has proven to be an effective anesthetic.

I recall the case of a woman who had bunionectomies on both feet. Those who had been through similar operations had warned her of the pain to be expected following this surgery. Because she was one of the local clergy wives, other clergy were notified of her operation, all being told that it was supposed to be rather painful. She received Holy Communion and the laying-on-of-hands before going in for surgery. I didn't see her until later that evening, when I asked her how she felt, and if there was much pain?

"Not a bit of pain—nothing. But I'd better not have any. Starting with the Holy Communion you gave me early this morning I have had around-the-clock visits from the clergy, and they all prayed for me. There was the Roman Catholic chaplain of the hospital here—the Episcopal bishop was in town and he came by with two other priests—oh yes, and the young Greek Orthodox priest was here too. No wonder I don't have any pain!"

She never did have any pain as a result of that operation, and though she was given crutches she never had to use them. Not only was there no pain but the surgery was a complete success, both cosmetically and functionally.

When a regular healing service is held in the church, people will come to participate and receive whatever ministrations are offered without informing the priest of their specific need. Many times people are in search of relief from pain and find help in the healing service. I have often been told by those who have been there that the healing services had sustained them as they were going through a difficult time. One person was in the custom of letting me know that the problem was pain and would point to the area on the head or neck which hurt the most. Like the case of the other man mentioned, she spoke of the feeling of heat, "like being under a heat lamp, but more intense." Though sensation may be felt in people receiving spiritual therapy, the majority of those who work in this field do not consider it to be important or necessary for healing. I mention it in passing because it is a phenomenon occasionally experienced by those receiving the laying-on-of-hands.

"Let Mommie kiss and make it better." Who hasn't heard this and who hasn't felt better when it happened to him? Remember what I said about the chief ingredient in healing? It is love, and mothers have known about it for a long time—and they've been using it with success. It's called God's anesthesia.

IX.
Varieties of Healing Experiences

There are more varieties of Christian healing than one can imagine. What St. Paul says in his first letter to Corinth seems to apply to the whole ministry of spiritual healing. "Now there are diversities of gifts, but the same Spirit. And there are differences of administrations, but the same Lord. And there are diversities of operations, but it is the same God which worketh all in all" (I Corinthians 12:4-6). In this chapter I'm going to take the liberty of touching on a number of different kinds of healing experiences to demonstrate the infinite variety of God's healing gifts.

There was the case of Peg. She taught me the value of the dedicated lay persons' own ministry in healing. One day my daughters were off for the day with their favorite Sunday School teacher. When they arrived home Linda shouted to me, "Dad, Donna got.her finger shut in the car door," and before I could respond she added, "but It's O.K. now because Peg prayed for it just as soon as it happened." Donna arrived to show me that her finger was really all right. "That's right, Dad, it sure hurt when the door closed on it, but Peg just took it in her hands and said a prayer and the pain left." A crisis came for Peg when she became pregnant. The idea of the pregnancy was fine, but a medical examination revealed that there was a tumor in her womb of considerable size. To remove the tumor would be to abort the fetus and to leave it there would make the birth of the child quite impossible. She said to the doctor, "Let me work on this for a while before you decide to do anything." She "worked on it" in this manner: she informed me and all other interested in healing to pray for the removal of the tumor and for the health of the unborn child. She pointed out that she had a deadline to make: her next monthly appointment with the doctor. When the month was up, the doctor was aided in making a decision by what he found upon examining her. The tumor, which had been described as being "about the size of a pear," was nowhere to be found. It had completely disappeared. When the child was born later on, the doctor referred to her as his "miracle baby." You can see how having someone like Peg around strengthened me in my own work with the sick. Such people as these are invaluable to the priest's healing ministry.

I have spoken about the need for closer ties between the medical men and the Church's ministers of healing. The following case is one that might have been more successful if there had been a consultation between the doctor and me. I received a cry for help from a young mother who was puffed up from a violent allergic reaction. He eyes were so swollen that she could scarcely see. The itching was unbearable and her whole body was inflamed. The problem was a complicated one. She had acquired an infection for which there is a specific remedy. It was after she had received the drug which was a specific for this infection that she had the allergic reaction. The cure was worse than the disease. My heart went out to her when I saw her, she was so miserable. Her face and eyes seemed to be the most obvious area of distress, so I placed my hands over her cheeks and eyelids and asked God to send relief. Relief came fast, in fact right away, as the swelling drained form her face and her eyes opened wide before me. It was a wonderful experience and we were both thankful. However, I received a call later on that night from her husband. On orders from her doctor she had taken more medicine and had a bad reaction again. I did not interfere because she was his patient and I assumed he was doing what he considered best for her. I couldn't help feeling, though, that a consultation might have been in order. She did recover successfully from both conditions and even though she had returned to the allergic problem she never forgot the reality and the rapidity of God's answer to our prayers.

Sometimes I feel that we try too hard to bring about a spiritual healing. It's like the athlete who over-trains, who wants so badly to win that he ends up by losing. My wife had a lot of discomfort from a plantar wart on the sole of her foot. I tried the laying-on-of-hands method of spiritual healing but nothing seemed to happen. Then I had to take a trip to a conference, and took along Emily Gardiner Neal's first book, *A Reporter Finds God Through Spiritual Healing*[1] to read on the plane. I came to the section where she reported noticing warts being removed from a boy at a healing service, and thought of Jo's plantar wart. I thought, "Maybe I've been trying too hard—it should be more responsive than this." I decided to pray for its removal right then and as the jet sailed through the sky my prayers were focused on a problem miles away. A week later, when I returned from the conference she met me at the airport.

"You know what?"

"Yes, the wart is gone, isn't it?"

"Why yes, but how did you know? I wondered if you'd been trying something different. The whole thing just dropped out, all in one piece. What did you do that was different?"

"I stopped trying so hard. I just prayed nice and easy while I was up there in the sky."

There is a common situation you find in many of the books on Christian healing. In the first place a medical diagnosis is made. On the basis of that examination, usually involving X-rays and other diagnostic tests, a certain course of action such as surgery is decided upon. Then the sick person receives some kind of spiritual ministration, such as the laying-on-of-hands, anointing, penance, the Holy Communion, or prayer alone. Another examination takes place and the doctors decide "some error has taken place" in the earlier diagnosis, so the operation is cancelled.

There was a child brought to me for prayers just before she was to be sent on the plane from Anchorage, Alaska, to San Francisco for heart surgery. Our prayers were for health and for the guidance of the physicians in charge. There was no operation. There was no need. The condition, diagnosed in Anchorage, was no longer found to be critical in San Francisco, just four hours away by plane.

Another time, a woman in my parish was rushed to the hospital with bleeding ulcers. Her case was considered bad enough to call for emergency surgery that evening. I managed to see her in the afternoon in order to pray for her and to talk with her about her condition. I told her that God might very well use surgery to effect a cure, but that He might choose to use other means to make her well. So I placed my hands over the area of discomfort and asked for healing. Her husband called me about seven that evening.

"They've called off the surgery, Father. She seemed so much better to them that they decided to take new pictures, and that made them change their minds. She told me to be sure and call you with the good news."

Pregnancies in women are so simple for some and so difficult for a few. There have been a number of instances when we applied spiritual healing to those undergoing a difficult pregnancy. Perhaps the most dramatic case was that of a woman who was losing her baby. Though her husband had been told by the doctor to prepare her for a miscarriage, she was convinced that I could help. He called, apologetically, and explained the circumstances to me, asking if I would come by to give her some comfort. I did drop by—and you know the rest. "Our" baby is quite a big boy now. Other women who have had trouble carrying babies develop anxieties and tensions in future pregnancies, and that tends to give them trouble. Whenever I hear of someone who is pregnant, particularly if there has been a history of difficulty, I place her name on the prayer list and encourage her to attend some of our healing services. I feel that has proved to be quite beneficial in many cases.

Concerning "differences in administrations" one item which is surely different is the use of the telephone in spiritual healing. Yet the telephone is often used, for distance does not inhibit God's healing rays from encircling the earth. A prayer group meets in New York and a sick person is healed in San Francisco. I pray while riding in a plane and a healing takes place elsewhere, on the ground. One of my favorite methods of praying for someone at a distance is to give the laying-on-of-hands to someone here in behalf of the sick person there. You may react the way the Episcopal priest did with Mrs. Neal, but I agree with her on this subject.

It's just ridiculous," he exploded, "to believe that anyone kneeling *here* can receive the laying on of hands for his Uncle Ed in Wisconsin." (This does sound ridiculous but, for that matter, how any intercession works is a great mystery of the Faith.)
My answer to the priest was that the laying on of hands received in this way is simply a form of intercessory prayer; when we receive for another, we simply bring the individual before God, praying that His healing power may be released and asking that we may be open channels for the love and grace of God in the lives of those for whom we pray.[2]

I have had too many satisfactory experiences with this type of intercessory prayer to toss it aside lightly. After having him attend one of our healing services and hearing some of our good results, I asked my brother, the doctor, what he thought of our program. He said, "If it works, don't knock it." And that is how I feel about the healing ministry.

Sometimes you encounter strange reactions from those who have been healed. Once, while I was in the sacristy, preparing for my eight o'clock Communion service, one of the men of the parish stumbled into the room, and with a groan, he slipped into a chair. I could see the look of pain on his face as he barely touched his leg.

"What's the matter with you, Douglas?" I asked.

Carefully, very carefully, he folded back his pant-leg and revealed a raw and ugly burn. The fluid was still oozing through the bandages. A worker in a foundry, he had come into contact with molten metal, and this was the result.

"Does it hurt?" I asked.

"You bet your sweet life it hurts—I can feel it throbbing now."

"I know I'm supposed to begin the service now, but that can wait a bit. There's no excuse for your having that pain any more."

Very lightly I placed my hands over the gauzed area and prayed for God to relieve his pain and bring about restoration to the damaged tissue. Then I entered the sanctuary and began the service. I didn't see Douglas after the Church service. My associate did seem him later on that week and found out that he was most unhappy with me. For not healing his burns? No. For making it worse? No. He was mad at me because it healed *too soon* and he had to return to work at least a week earlier than he had planned. He complained, "Because Fr. Miner healed me, the doctor said I could go back to work right away."

I had given him the laying-on-of-hands on Sunday. He had reported back to his doctor on Monday. The doctor was amazed at the condition of his leg and called it "a fantastic recovery." Then much to the chagrin of Douglas, the doctor released him to go back to work on the next day, Tuesday. As a result I was in the dog-house.

In my experience I have known burns to react most favorably to prayer therapy. I was familiar with one case of a young mother, who had second-and third-degree burns on her hand. Because she was the wife of a seminarian, the whole student body at the school concentrated on prayers for her recovery. The physician felt certain that skin grafting would be necessary. On the day she was to have her final examination to determine the necessity of skin grafts the doctor detected small islands of healthy tissue beginning to appear. He considered that a most unusual turn of events. As far as we knew, the only extra therapy applied was the concerted action of the seminarians in prayer.

Earlier I mentioned how often bone breaks have knit faster with spiritual therapy. I explained that fact to a young teen-age boy whose leg break was not healing properly. He had a deadline to meet. If his break did not show signs of healing in ten days they planned to re-set it and put a new cast on him. Just as I was about to lay hands upon him, he gave me the word.

"Now, Father, I don't want to be your first failure!"

Two weeks later I saw him in a church sitting in the congregation. When I caught his eye he grinned at me and held up his hand with the peace sign, which assured me that our bone-fracture record of speedy healings was still intact.

Sometimes God brings people together where there is a need—some action to be taken, some crisis to be averted. As I was driving along a busy turnpike and was still about 30 miles from home, a hitch hiker was getting out of a car ahead of me on the road. I felt a strong urgency to slow down, and when I did, I recognized the rider, who was in an Air Force uniform. He was a friend of the family. Naturally, he was glad to see my face as I stopped to pick him up.

When he got in my car I was surprised at his appearance. His hair was disheveled and his uniform was dirty. I could see that he was disturbed. He sat there silently for a while, and then the whole story came forth.

He was A.W.O.L. from an Air Force Base in Texas. He had hitch-hiked from there to this point in Massachusetts, thirty miles from home. Someone had written to him, informing him that his wife was seeing another man. In Texas he was thousands of miles from home and unable to do anything about this domestic situation. To compound matters he was away from his home for the first time. He would lie on his bunk and torture himself, thinking of his wife in the arms of some other man. The more he thought about it, the more agitated he became. He decided to do something about it.

As soon as he was released from the base on a weekend pass, he headed straight for home. As he pressed on, day after day closer to his mark, hateful thoughts possessed his thinking. He would kill them both. They didn't know he was coming. He would surprise them and put an end to their deceitful behavior.

He shared these thoughts with me as we drove closer and closer to his destination. Gradually he invited me into the conversation, giving me the opportunity to turn the thoughts from hate towards love and forgiveness. We continued to talk as in any normal counseling session, and as we did, he became more relaxed and less hostile.

As we approached his home, his worst suspicions proved to be true. The other man's car was parked in the driveway of his house. I looked at my young friend to see his reaction. He was calm, in control of his feelings and actions. He got out of the car, stepped to the front door and walked in. He was in there for some time as I continued to sit in my car in front of his house. I began to be quite uneasy.

There was no murder. Instead, when he finally came to the door he called to me to come in. Thus began the first of a series of counseling sessions which would eventually lead to the restoration of their marriage. Clearly, God entered into that situation, using me just in time to prevent a possible catastrophy.

That young man had traveled literally thousands of miles on a mission of hatred and vengeance only to be picked up thirty miles from home, by not only a friend of the family, but a minister as well. God brought us together, and gave us just enough time to discuss the problem before reaching his home. Riding along in the car together I prayed for guidance as he talked, and guidance came to me. "Praise God from whom all blessings flow." We must always be on the alert for God's signals to us, urging us to call on someone, to make a phone call, to write a letter. Looking back at our life experiences, haven't we all had times when the person we went to see, phoned or wrote, informed us that *at that very moment* they needed our help?

One of my brother's friends had a most unusual experience. He drove for a car pool and each day made a pick-up at 7:30 in the morning. One day as he arrived at his friend's home there was no response when he honked the horn. When he went to the front door and rang the bell, nobody responded. He pounded on the back door. Still nothing. As he checked out the house further he noted signs that indicated to him that the family was still in the house. The car and the children's bikes were in the garage. The shades were drawn in the bedrooms. Sensing that something was drastically wrong, he broke one of the small windows in the back door, reached in, turned the knob, and let himself in. As soon as he opened the door he could smell gas. He rushed to the kitchen stove, found gas escaping from one of the jets and turned it off. He dashed to the bedrooms where he found the man and wife and their children all unconscious. He quickly opened the other doors and windows and called for an ambulance. Before the ambulance could arrive he had managed to get all the family outdoors in the fresh air and bring them to partial consciousness. When he had completed all this he glanced at his watch. It was 7:30, the time he was supposed to show up at that home. For some unexplained reason he had arrived at his stop fifteen minutes early,something he had never done previously,he was later told by the attending physician that his being just those fifteen minutes early had probably made the difference between the family's living or dying.

He told my brother that he felt that he was needed there

even before he had reached the house. He had experienced a strong sense of urgency, which made him start for work early even though he could see no tangible reason for his actions. After it was all over he thanked God for giving him the chance to save their lives. God had given him an opportunity and he had acted upon it. How do we have such opportunities but—because we do not recognize them as such—fail to act upon them? Though all needs are not as crucial as this, it is common for God to lead us to places where we can help. There are many times when he speaks to us in this way but because we are not "tuned in" we don't get the message. If we are alert and receptive we can hear his directives loud and clear.

At the beginning of this chapter I spoke of the infinite variety of God's healing gifts. Living prayerfully—keeping a hot line open between you and God—leads you to an infinite variety of opportunities for service. Not only do you get sent to meet emergency situations such as those mentioned above, but also you can be guided to new work, sent to different churches or communities where your special talents are needed. That doesn't mean that you will always immediately know what God has in store for you. Sometimes you may have to wait for him to unfold him plan before you can understand.

When my wife Joan died, in a way I felt as though my life was also at an end. Our daughters were married and living away. Daily I had shared in her struggle; when it came to an end for her, I felt that I had "had it" too. There I was, living alone for the first time in years. I wondered what future there was for me. I never could have dreamed how the hand of God was at that very time at work, in fact, had been all the time in a way that would eventually awaken me to all sorts of new challenges.

Years ago in Alaska I had met and worked with a young woman on the program committee of the Armed Services YMCA in Anchorage. She was on the staff, and after two years accepted an assignment at the U.S.O. in Naples, Italy. We gave her a royal Alaskan send-off and thought we probably wouldn't be seeing her again. A couple of years later I left Alaska for work in California. While we were living there, one night Marga's picture appeared in the local paper as the new Program Director of the U.S.O. in Monterey. Joan and I got in touch with her and we were glad to hash over the good old times in Alaska. Three years later Joan had died and Marga was off again on a new assignment to Newport, Rhode Island. Again, I had no idea that I'd ever see her again. I had no reason to be in that part of the country. My work was in California. My married daughters were in Alaska. The next year a strange thing happened as a result of my mother's death. My mother died while living with my brother in Colorado. The family plot was in the East, however, so the funeral service and burial were to be held there. I shared the service with the Rector my mother best knew in the East. Before I returned home to California he had invited me to come back East and work with him. His parish was in Warwick, Rhode Island.

I accepted and, as you must have already surmised, Marga and I met again; in time we were married. It was not long before all signs seem to point to the North, to Alaska, where I had already had a fruitful ministry and where new challenges were beckoning. I share this story with you to point to God, not as a match-maker, but as the Father who knows us and our needs intimately and helps us to fulfill them. He knows our talents and if we agree to accept his orders he will direct us to work opportunities awaiting our special abilities, as well as to help-mates who can assist us in our life and work.

When you ask any ordained minister why he chose the ministry for his life's work he will tell you that he felt *called* to that service. In other words, he came to the conclusion that God had that work in mind for him. As He said to Jeremiah, "Before I formed you in the womb I knew you, and before you were born I consecrated you; I appointed you a prophet to the nations" (Jeremiah 1:5, R.S.V.). It is that same conviction about being called by God to His ministry that leads us into other paths, other varieties of expression and service in the world. The healing ministry is but one of those expressions of God's presence in our lives. As discussed in this chapter alone, it has many diverse means of operation, "but it is the same God which worketh all in all." On one occasion God's presence may be seen through the laying-on-of-hands and the subsequent healing of disease. It may appear as the elimination of pain or the soothing calm that comes with peace of mind. It can come by means of counseling, where the counselor is led to the need and guided in what he must say. It can be the hand of God healing the broken hearted and leading them to new challenges for service. It can be the all-knowing God, bringing people together to new partnerships in the service of their fellow man. God calls not only men, to the ordained ministry, but also to specific acts of service at any time. We must keep listening.

X.
Who Can Be Healed?

Who can be healed spiritually? Are there any limits to the healing power of God? Are the gifts of healing restricted to Christians? Are the blessings of healing restricted to those who believe? Does it make any difference for healing if a person is in good standing in his church? What about healings among primitive peoples? What about pagans?

You can well imagine that the vast majority of people I have dealt with have been Christians, members of established churches. In general those who assist in the prayer groups and attend the services are the people most likely to request our ministrations and prayers when they are sick themselves. As a result, practically all the illustrations I have given in this book have involved Christians, most of whom were members of the Episcopal Church.

There are no limits, however, set on God's power to heal. Healing gifts are not restricted to Christians or kinds of Christians. From New Testament times until this day the gift of healing was offered not because a person's church or standing in that church, but because the person had a need: he was sick.

If there is one condition that often seems to exist as a requirement for healing, it is that the sick person believe. Even here, however, we know that sometimes the sick person was not consulted, did not even know he was being prayed for. Other times the one who was ill appeared not to believe—but someone else did.

Because belief (someone's belief) is one of the requirements for healing, usually believing Christians have been the most responsive to healing prayers in my experience. Many times it has been necessary for me to educate them briefly on what spiritual healing is in today's church. Often just the simplest of explanations is sufficient for them to understand enough to want prayers and other ministrations. On a number of occasions it was the illness and healing ministry that brought the sick person to a new awareness and belief in God.

It has not been uncommon for me to have responsive healing results with those who refer to themselves as "backsliders." Some of our baptized members on the church rolls are not even "C & E members" (Christmas and Easter). Nevertheless, I have long been convinced that faith or belief often has little to do with perfunctory acts of worship or church attendance. When a person has no church affiliation he will suffer from a lack of information about Christian life and practice, but that does not mean that he does not believe, that he does not have a faith in God. In fact, sometimes we find those who are unchurched or nominal members to possess a strong belief as well as a genuine commitment to serve God and their fellow-man.

In Alaska there are significant numbers of Eskimos, Indians, and Aleuts. Those people come from cultures which have embraced some form of religion since their beginnings. Though most of these native Alaskans are Christians today, their faith has remained simple and direct, with a genuine feeling for the nearness and reality of God's presence. Prayer is a very real thing to them, something they take seriously, and it is easy for them to accept healing as a natural result of prayer.

A story about one of our Eskimo delegates to a conference illustrates how prayer is a natural and practical part of their life. He had flown from Alaska to Seattle, where he was to meet one of our Alaskan clergy delegates and go on to the convention with him. A stranger in the city, he soon became lost among the many pedestrians on the streets. Feeling awkward about being lost, he hesitated to ask anyone for help. When he did ask, it meant nothing to the people he asked.

"You know Father Hall? You know where is Father Hall? I looking for Father Hall."

This is how he explained it to me:

"Nobody know Father Hall; so I think, what I do when I lost on trail back home? I pray. I lost in this place so I kneel on street here too. I say, 'God, help me find Father Hall.' I get up and look who I see coming across street shouting my name—Father Hall!"

The belief in God's nearness and availability has long been with those people. Prayers of thanksgiving are a regular part of the hunt when a whale has been killed. They know God has provided the food for their nurture. Years ago their very survival depended on a successful hunt. Today, though they have other sources of food, they still give public thanks to God.

Young Alaskan natives are now well educated and becoming sophisticated. With parts of this great land being divided and developed, they "want a piece of the action." They are coming into their own in business, politics, and the issues of human rights. Let us pray that, as they find their place in modern America, they don't abandon the devout prayer and belief habits of their elders.

One instance of healing prayers with those outside of the Christian faith meant a great deal to me and the whole family involved. The son of one of my Jewish friends had been under treatment for a rare condition. He was receiving the best medical treatment available, but continued to go down hill. Nothing seemed to help. I could see the concern in his father's face and I wanted to do something for him.

"Saul, we've put your son's name on the prayer list at our church. Tell him that we are praying for him to get well."

He reacted most appreciatively when he heard this news and seemed very interested as I continued.

"There's just one more thing I'd like to do. I'd like to meet the boy and talk with him about healing and how prayer helps. I realize that you are Jewish and have your own beliefs, but the God of Moses and the Prophets is my God too, and the Jesus to whom I owe allegiance was brought up in a Jewish home. I think I might be able to help the boy. I'd like to try, anyway."

I made my call, and met his son, who was about 13 years of age. I talked to the boy within the context of his own religion. That was not difficult to do, because of the evidence of spiritual healing in the Old Testament. I was careful to point out to him the way in which his doctors were likewise carrying out God's purposes. As we talked, a rapport developed between us that was warm and friendly and it was an easy thing to give him the laying-on-of-hands. It was a nice experience and a sharing of love between me, the boy, and his whole family. He began to respond to his treatments. The last I heard, he was still improving. Something more came out of this than the boy's own physical improvement. As I laid hands upon him and prayed aloud to the God of Abraham, Isaac, and Jacob—his God and my God—I felt a tremendous kinship to that Jewish boy, through Christ. And the love of the God of Moses and the Prophets filled the room.

We find evidences of spiritual healing in all of the world's great religions and among primitive religions as well. In India there are holy men, who have a reputation for healing the sick. Even in the most elementary societies we find the shaman or witch doctor, who is a kind of primitive medic and priest combined. Faulty and imperfect as these religions may have been, the simple faith and trust of the people involved, and God's responding love, often brought about right results. Though not recognized by name, Christ and his healing hands have indeed given healing to the sick, who approached him in the only way they could understand.

When the Church first sent medical missionaries to work among those in foreign lands, their principal work in healing was among the pagan peoples. It was not necessary for them to teach non-Christians that there was a God with the power to heal. Rather, it was their task to teach them what they believed to be his true name and nature. He was not an evil spirit who needed to be appeased, but a loving father who cared for his people and wanted them to be well. It was often the work among the sick by the medical missionaries which paved the path for later teaching and conversion to the Christian faith. Conversion or no, it has always been the standard practice of Christian missionaries to offer medical assistance and to pray for *all the people.*

Disease is something that affects human beings, animals, birds, fish, and plant-life. Doctors of veterinary medicine use many of the same pharmaceuticals and biologicals for the treatment of their patients as do the physicians for human beings. They employ much of the same therapy and surgical techniques as well. They show the same concern and care for the treatment of these animals as doctors show for human patients.

Though I am not prepared to give any real evidence of spiritual healing among the animals, I do feel led to make some observations on the subject. In the first place, if it is possible for man to love his pets, we know that it must likewise be true of God, for the perfect love of God is far more encompassing than man's imperfect love. All of the creatures upon this earth were placed here by God and loved by Him. In Genesis I:25 we read, "And God made the beasts of the earth according to their kinds and the cattle according to their kinds, and everything that creeps upon the ground according to its kind. And God saw that it was good" (R.S.V.). If they too are God's creatures, looked upon by Him with satisfaction, I am of the opinion that the use of prayer brings results among animals as well as human beings.

Whether that is true or not, I do know that pets—dogs, cats, hamsters, rabbits and other domestic creatures—probably are prayed for as much as, or more than, human beings. Let's face it. People are close to their pets. I saw the health of an old lady disintegrate when her pet cat of some 18 years died. Countless households have seemed painfully empty when the pet dog, a constant companion for years, finally died. What child has had a sick pet and has not prayed for him? And why not? For these are God's own creatures, placed on this earth by him for a purpose. That purpose has often been to bring companionship and happiness to many a home. Naturally, it is a much more difficult thing to demonstrate God's healing power in animals than in humans. We can only observe and form our opinions from what we see.

Like most people who have had pets since childhood, I can't remember a time when I didn't pray for any that were ill. I won't even try to estimate whether I had a high rate of recovery or not. However, I did have one experience that stands out in my mind as unusual. I had a small Siamese kitten given to me, who was the runt of the litter and not very well from birth. When she was about six minths old she contracted some illness and began to fail badly. She refused to eat, was losing weight, and finally became so weak that she couldn't walk across the floor. It was Sunday afternoon; I took her with me in the car and tried to find a veterinarian who was working, but I did not succeed.

I sat in my car outside the closed office and looked at the helpless little thing, huddled against the back of the seat. I picked her up. She didn't have the strength to stand in my hands. As she lay there I began to talk to God, informally, just as I would to another person.

"Lord, this is one of your little creatures. She's so sick and I don't know what to do to help her. The vet isn't here and I'm afraid she won't last until morning. I know You can heal her, Lord, so enter into her now and make her well. Amen."

After my prayer I drove towards home, thinking of how Saint Francis loved the animals, and of how God must love them too. It didn't happen until I reached home again. I got out of the car, took her in my hands and opened the door of my house. Then came the surprise. The limp form in my hand stood up, leaped to the floor, and ran through the living room and out into the kitchen. When I caught up with her she was greedily drinking all the milk in the saucer. When she finished with that she turned and attacked the cat food in the other dish. She was no longer sick—she had been healed.

As I said previously I have no knowledge of the extent of divine healing in animals. They certainly are given a large measure of what the ancients called the "vis medicatrix naturae" (healing power of nature) as is evidenced by their natural recovery from injuries as well as diseases. Of this I am certain, that it is well within God's province and capacity to heal them and it is my opinion that He does.

Much attention is being given today to the importance and care of all of God's living things, not just man and the larger animals, but also the whole multitude of living things, including insects and plant life. We are now learning how important the health of all living things is to the health and well-being of man himself.

Pollution of streams and oceans brings disease and death to types of plant life scarcely visible to man's eyes and hardly noticed previously. Plankton, the small animal and plant organisms that float and drift in the water, are now known to be responsible for important health-giving oxygen. When these different kinds of plant life are destroyed through ignorance or wanton pollution, the balance of nature is thrown off.

A word now receiving much attention is *ecology,* defined in the dictionary as "that branch of biology which treats of the relation of organisms and their environment." Ecology has now come to public attention because the health and welfare of mankind is seriously threatened. Some scientists say that man is already doomed by his polluted air and streams and the destruction of life forms necessary for his survival. Others say that there is still a chance for man's future if we reverse the trend towards destruction and change the direction to conservation and restoration of God's creations. Here in Alaska we feel a strong sense of the necessity of conservation of our beautiful country and the bountiful wildlife we have. That is why so much care is being given to the proper methods of extracting such natural resources as oil and mineral deposits found here.

Christians have two reasons for joining the fight against pollution and maintaining the proper care of our environment. The first of these reasons is the responsibility put into our hands by God at the beginning of creation. Again from Genesis I:29 we read, "And God said, 'Behold I have given you every plant yielding seed which is upon the face of all the earth, and every tree with seed in its fruit; you shall have them for food. And to every beast of the earth, and to every bird of the air, and to everything that creeps on the earth, *everything that has the breath of life,* I have given every green plant for food.' And it was so. And God saw everything that he had made, and behold, *it was very good.*"

When God created man and made him steward over His earth, His animals and birds and all other living things, the natural state of things was very good. As children of God it is incumbent upon us to do all that we can to restore our environment to its natural state of goodness. It is indeed sinful for man to continue with the careless plundering of the wilderness and the living things which dwell there. It is sinful for us to continue to pollute the air and the streams because it destroys important life forms necessary for the balance of nature.

The second reason for our being interested in ecology and conservation is tied in with out interest in healing and health. It doesn't make sense to pray for health in individuals at the same time that we help to undermine everybody's health with our pollution. We who are involved in the healing movement must do our part whenever possible to join in this crusade to protect our environment from things harmful to our health.

We know that when we call upon God to restore us to health it is not just a matter of letting Him do it all. It is up to us to do our part in responding to his healing power. We must get our exercise, proper sleep and food, and otherwise cooperate with God, so we don't impede any healing process he has begun within us. I remember the lady with an alcoholic problem, who was asking me to pray for her recovery. Every so often she would excuse herself and go into the bathroom. When she would return her condition would be worse and she would ask me to pray for her again.

My suspicions proved to be correct when I entered the bathroom and found a bottle hidden there. No wonder the prayers seemed ineffective. How could she expect the prayers to work when she continued to pollute herself with alcohol at the very same time? We do this sort of thing all the time. We ask to be relieved of emphysema, then go and have another cigarette. We allow refuse to pour into our streams, then wonder why there are no longer any fish in those waters.

We who have been made stewards of God's earth, with all its living things, have a solemn obligation to protect and nurture the things of nature. We who have received the call to heal must realize that in order to achieve health for mankind, we must maintain a health-giving environment. Yes, God made this earth, and it was very good when He turned it over to us. For His sake and for our health's sake we must make it very good again.

XI.
Where Do We Go
From Here?

When Jesus Christ sent forth his disciples, he commissioned them to preach and teach the good news of the forgiveness of sins and the redemption of mankind. To be saved and to be forgiven is to be healed in the whole person. That is what Christ wants for all of us. That is why He came into the world, why He gave His life that we might live. That is why He sent men forth to preach and to heal. And each one of us who has been baptized is challenged to "take up his cross" and follow Him, personally assisting in His ministry; a part of that ministry is spiritual healing.

How do we go about that ministry, particularly if the idea is new to us? In the first place we can begin with ourselves. We can strive for health in our own lives. We should make a personal inventory of our lives, how we have lived, how we are measuring up today, and where we should be tomorrow. We must rid ourselves of all our sins; all bitterness, resentment, prejudice, hatred, and false pride. We must purge ourselves of stored up feelings of guilt through honest confession and amendment of life, asking Christ to enter our hearts and minds and cleanse us of all sin.

Next, we should get acquainted with all that is going on in the field of spiritual healing through reading the Bible and some of the very helpful books that are written as testimonies of healing experiences in our time. There are a number of periodicals on this subject, also.

We must seek out others with whom we can share in that ministry. We must find the group that has been referred to as the loving congregation, for that is the group that is indispensable to an effective ministry to the sick. The special charismatic gifts of a few celebrated spiritual healers are not as important to a healing ministry as the supportive power generated by a dedicated prayer group. All that is needed are the two or three faithful ones gathered in His name; where they are to be found, He is also to be found in the midst of them, and where He is, you will find healing.

It is the concerted action of the prayer group that generates sacramental healing. John Large explains the roles of the priest and congregation very nicely:

> The loving congregation, on the other hand, need be in possession of no extraordinary gifts whatsoever. As a matter of fact, the law of averages clearly indicates the total absence, by and large, of any such talents. But whether the group is a foregathering of untutored peasants or of intellectual giants or of remarkably gifted mystics, this loving congregation has reverently come together simply to *evoke* the healing Spirit which the officiating priest or minister, acting as their spokesman, will then *mediate* sacramentally, as he was ordained to do.[2]

It is important to know that we need no special gifts of our own, that the Holy Spirit can lead us to do things far beyond our normal capacities, because we do it in His name. You may find that there is a prayer fellowship already in existence in your church, one that meets regularly to offer prayers for the sick. There may be a healing service in which the minister gives the laying-on-of-hands for the sick or annointing with oil for health. Go and participate in those services and share in that fellowship. And if it isn't possible to meet with them you can still share in their intercessions for others by keeping your prayer list at home and joining with them from a distance.

Finally, be unafraid to accept the command to heal the sick. Think positively and remember that you are never alone in that endeavor. As you step up to the bedside of someone who is ill, remember that the power of the entire prayer group is with you and you already know Who is in the midst of the prayer group. And when you pray, pray with expectancy, knowing that it is God's desire that we all have healthy, happy lives. Finish eacy prayer with a "thank-you," for you know that as soon as you start your prayer God has already acted upon it.

The main thing to remember is that *the healing ministry is important.* It is not just a nice gesture to comfort people—it works! In the vernacular of today, healing is for real. It is important to the sick that we in the Church keep active in the healing ministry. It is important to ourselves and to our own health of body, mind, and soul. Most of all, it is important to God, who wants us to be well.

Every prayer offered for the recovery of a sick person is a part of the healing ministry and a form of spiritual healing that can be practiced by anyone, anywhere. If that ministry is to be fully expressed, however, and is to involve as many people as possible, it should become a formal part of the life of a parish, through the organization of prayer groups and healing services.

Any such formal expression of the healing ministry, of course, requires the assent and cooperation of both clergy and laymen to be successful. Many of us, including many clergy, are unfamiliar with spiritual healing; being human, most of us tend to be indifferent, if not actively hostile, to things we know nothing about. So the first practical step you can take toward initiating a formal healing ministry in your parish is to talk about spiritual healing, with your pastor, with members of the congregation. Chances are that you will find several others who know something about spiritual healing and who are interested in organizing prayer groups or healing services. You will find some people who know little about spiritual healing but who are open to it and interested in hearing about it.

With the help of a sympathetic pastor, a few laymen can organize a formal prayer group. Where there is a need for a more public form of healing ministry, any clergyman, with support from his congregation, can introduce healing services.

I have learned that there is no set pattern for a healing service. That is also true of a prayer group. The things that seem to work fine in one situation do not necessarily prove effective in another.

In many places the Holy Communion service is the setting used for the weekly healing service, with laying-on-of-hands or annointing with oil administered following the reception of the Sacrament, or perhaps offered after the completion of the service. There are advantages and disadvantages to the choice of Holy Communion as the main body for a healing service.

One advantge is the fact that there is a ready-made congregation in some churches. The parishioners are accustomed to having a regular week-day service of Holy Communion and will be present to offer intercessions, hear a talk on healing and receive an invitation to receive healing in their own lives. As time goes on the minister and the people gain more confidence and become less timid about participating in the healing aspects of these services. I say minister as well as people, because the ordained clergy often are not sure of themselves in the healing ministry and literally are learning along with the congregation. My own experience bears that out.

I chose the Holy Communion as the place to begin my healing services for the above reasons. We had a small number of regular attendants and had a long history of offering prayers for the sick at those Communion services. Then one day I made the big move: I offered laying-on-of-hands to any in the congregation who desired healing in their lives. They just looked at me and I began to feel ill at ease. I felt even more self-conscious when nobody came to the altar rail to receive the laying-on-of-hands. Following the service not one person mentioned anything to me about healing. They were talkative all right, but about everything else but healing: the weather, the bazaar, carefully avoiding any mention of something I regarded as new and bold, a healing ministry in our parish. I felt terrible. After months of thinking about it, praying about it, I finally took the step and offered them the gift of healing. Nobody even wanted it! They didn't even want to talk about it. It was not my day!

The next time around was better. A visitor from another parish, someone familiar with the practice, came forth for the laying-on-of-hands and upon seeing that, one of my regulars came up and joined her. We were on the way. As time went on others began to respond to the invitation and we all started to grow in the experience and knowledge of God's healing ministry.

Gradually individuals started to come to me following the service to discuss their needs and problems—to discuss healing. Others began reporting to me the positive results of healing in their lives or in the lives of others for whom we had been praying. Things began to happen. I became braver, and the people became braver, and we started to become the loving congregation, gathered to do God's work in the healing ministry.

Two things developed naturally to add strength to our services of healing. The first was the addition of a prepared talk on the subject of healing at each service. That proved helpful in more than one way: it forced me to study more on the subject and it gave the members of the congregation regular instruction on a topic that had been neglected during their own Christian education.

The second characteristic of our service, which developed on its own, came from the people. It was the practice of sharing and witnessing the reality of healing in their lives and in the lives of others. It happened this way. I had just finished my healing instruction and was about to return to the Communion service when one of the women present interrupted me.

"I'm sorry, Father, but I just have to say something to all of you. It just has to be said. I'm healed. I've been healed of asthma!"

At first no one said a thing. They looked with surprise, and perhaps with some disbelief. But as they continued to look at the expression of joy and thanksgiving on the face of their friend they began to have an awareness that something great had happened here.

I had forgotten about the incident until that moment. The witnessing lady came up to me during the coffee hour after the church services and asked me to pray for her. She was gasping for breath. I quickly went into the church with her and found out that she was in the midst of an asthma attack.

''Give . . . laying-on-of-hands . . . please, Father . . . please," she managed to get out as she knelt down at the altar rail. I placed my hands on her head and began to pray for her relief, for her health. Very soon the short, violent struggling for breath began to change to full and even breathing and she became calm. Because of activity in the parish hall I had to leave and did not see her again until she came to the week-day service. She felt that she had to come and share with us her wonderful experience.

After that day sharing became a common feature of the healing service in that church. In addition to testimonies which were made concerning our own experiences, we had reports on the persons on our prayer list. The "Prayer Board" was something that worked bery well in my church in Seaside, California. It all started when I brought in a large classroom chalk-board and wrote the names of the sick ones being offered to God in prayer. I just happened to leave it in the church until Sunday morning. Before I could remove it, someone added another name, so I left it there. During the service I told the members of the congregation what we had used it for. Following the worship others came forward and

added more names. Needless to say, it became a permanent
fixture in that parish. It was our Prayer Board. We used it not
only for the sick but for those traveling, for those desiring
guidance, for the secret prayers of many. Being near an Army
Post we had a number of servicemen who left our area for
combat duty. When they left their names were placed on the
board. Whenever one returned, we asked him to come
forward and erase his name, after which we offered a prayer
of thanksgiving. Though it was a small congregation, it was
difficult for me to keep track of all the names on the board,
for there was seldom a time when there were less than 100
names written there.

For that place at that time, the large chalk-board filled the
bill. I have not had it so successfully used in other
congregations, though I have used one elsewhere. That is
what I meant at the beginning of this chapter when I said
that there are no rigid rules to follow in setting up a healing
service. The service I have been describing was one that grew
out of a regular week-day service of the Lord's Supper. I
mentioned previously that there are disadvantages in using
the Holy Communion as the setting for a healing service.
When one uses a liturgical service such as the Communion,
the congregation tends to follow denominational lines. That
is certainly all right, but in many situations the healing
service is being offered to fill a community need. If that is
the case the approach must be ecumenical, using a service
that any Christian can follow with a little guidance from the
leader.

Time is often a factor, as in a noon-day service downtown.
There, a short service, involving some prayers and Scripture
reading, a short talk on the subject of healing, followed by
the laying-on-of-hands or annointing, might be most appro-
priate. You don't always get what you want at first.
Sometimes it takes some experimenting, some trial and error,
before a service jells.

If someone were to ask me what I thought needed to be

accomplished first in order to have a successful healing
ministry in a church, I should say, "one must develop a
climate for healing." Healing can be found everywhere in
God's creation and certainly in the Church. However, as
plants flourish in the proper climate with the right kind of
care and nurture, so does spiritual healing: it flourishes when
the climate is right.

In my work in the church I have been in many different
places. There have been times when the healing emphasis in
my ministry was weak or scarcely visible. There were other
times when the conditions or the climate were apparently
ideal, and it became the dominant tone in my total ministry.
One such period in my life occurred during the three years
my wife was sick with cancer. The entire congregation was
brought into that experience and gave proof of their love and
evidence of the power generated by prayer. Their prayers
created such stores of energy that we were actually lifted up
high enough to meet and conquer all we were called upon to
face. She was truly made strong in the midst of her weakness
and I was given strength in the Spirit to carry on my
ministry. In the end, when people went to her funeral they
couldn't cry, because there was too much of a feeling of life
and victory about the service. When we come face to face
with a triumph we do not wish to weep.

Following her death I stayed on in the parish for about a
year before moving on to new work, and during that time the
healing ministry remained strong. Even in victory a clergyman is human and subject to weakness; during some of
those lonely times it was the loving congregation who kept
the fires going and supplied the energy for their priest's
ministrations. I think that is important for all congregations
to remember: their prayers are continually needed to sustain
and strengthen their pastors, for there are numerous
occasions when the minister feels alone or discouraged or just
plain frustrated, trying to do what is right.

In moving away from the congregation which had stood by

me, prayed for me, and fortified my total ministry, I had some adjustments to make. As I said before, each situation is different, requiring other approaches and new solutions. In the process of moving on to new endeavors my kind of ministry changed. I found myself called upon to aid on diocesan healing commissions and to work with others in setting up healing programs. Wherever the healing program was faltering I observed the same deficiency: a lack of proper climate.

It takes a number of different elements working together to create a climate in which healing will flourish. It is not easy to find what is missing in a situation. On the surface everything seems to be all right for an ongoing healing service and prayer group ministry. The minister says he believes in spiritual healing. He visits the hospital regularly and prays for the sick. The prayer group members are given their lists and undoubtedly use them. Those who attend the services tell you that they approve of this emphasis, but still, something is wrong. Nothing really is happening there.

Then after you have been around them long enough you begin to wonder if they believe in healing—*really.* The minister says he does believe in healing but makes a great to-do about "when it's the will of God." Also, you may find out that his main emphasis in visiting the sick is on seeing them out of this world rather than gaining for them an extension of time. He gives the Communion and the Unction, but primarily as acts preparing them for death. A member of the prayer group mentions someone's name and adds, "it's a terminal case," and the others respond with, "what a shame." Others attending the services say they believe in healing and at the same time hide the fact that they are going to the hospital for surgery.

All of these things have their place. The clergy do have a valid ministry to prepare people for death. Many times "terminal" is merely a description passed on by a family member to the prayer group. It is also true that some persons are shy about asking help for themselves. But when such attitudes are generally characteristic and set the tone of the whole group, that the climate isn't right for a positive healing program. Some of the poeple who make healing most difficult are clergy and lay people who say they believe in healing but then go on to add all sorts of qualifications before it can happen.

"Of course I believe in healing, particularly in psychological cases. Well, when it's strictly a physical ailment, it's different. That's why we have doctors, isn't it?"

I remember one experience that occurred in a church office involving three professional church workers. My assistant was complaining of a severe backache. He had taken some aspirin for it, but it was still giving him trouble and I suggested the laying-on-of-hands for his relief. He gladly consented, and while he sat there I prayed for him. My Christian Education Director, who had been observing all this, waited until I was through and then immediately added her advice.

"Now get yourself out of that chair and over to the doctor's office right away!"

She didn't even wait for him to stand up and see if the pain had left. She was unaware of how completely she demonstrated her lack of faith until I looked at her and said, "After all, you've got to give God a fighting chance!"

We all broke out in laughter at that point and she said, "But I really do believe in spiritual healing—I'm just worried about his back."

We believe, but we don't believe, and that hesitation or doubt is often enough negativity to discourage or impede or prevent some act of healing from taking place.

When that attitude becomes the attitude of the clergy and laity involved with the church's healing ministry, the climate is not right. Healings may occur and may not even be recognized as such by the group, or even by those healed. I remember a lady who had a complete turnabout in her

condition soon after receiving the laying-on-of-hands. On my
first visit to her following her recovery she surprised me with
her words.

"I'm all better. Aren't antibiotics wonderful?"

"They sure are," I replied. "They are provided by the same
God who answers our prayers and strengthens us in other
ways."

I have spent some time with those things which make for a
poor climate. We need to know about them, but it is even
more important that we know those elements that contribute
to a positive climate for a healing ministry.

One of the first things to look for in developing the right
climatic conditions is a note of joyful optimism on the part
of those involved. The positive and happy voice of our friend
who had to testify that she had been healed spread to the
others. Someone had dared to forget about normal inhibi-
tions and speak out the joyful truth. That act broke down
the walls of reserve in others.

We are fearful of so many things: afraid they'll think we're
naive, afraid they'll think we are not intelligent, afraid they
might make fun of us. We are afraid of what they think and
perhaps they are afraid of what we may think. All this fear
comes from a lack of trust. People live in a state of anxiety
for fear of being put down or having their feelings hurt. They
have things to share but because of their fears they say
nothing.

All this takes us back to the "loving congregation." Love
casts out fear—love is kind. When the climate is right the
congregation loves, has compassion, understands, forgives,
and makes it possible for anyone to trust without fear of
some kind of rejection. You know the climate is right when
you are loved and give love in return, are trusted and give
trust in return.

Before you can have the kind of conditions present for
healing you must have people around you who believe. Belief
is a normal requisite for spiritual healing. In my first example

in this book, of the mother in a coma, *my* faith was weak, but the daughter believed. In the case of the small boy who was apparently dying, most everyone had given up—his parents, friends, and the medical staff—but *he* believed and *I* believed. The believer may be a prayer group, either present or miles away; it may be a child, who loves and cares and prays and expects. When surrounded by such as these—believers, witnesses, who have either experienced healing personally in their lives or have seen it in others—a pastor can scarcely keep from having a dynamic healing ministry.

One thing we should consider when planning to begin a healing service in a community is the kind of image we shall project. The uninstructed and ill-informed may react with scoffing and disbelief, uneasiness, or fear. It is not at all unusual for people involved in a healing ministry to be regarded as "a bunch of weirdos" to be avoided. That is especially true where the healing services may reach a high emotional pitch. Also, practices that may appear strange to outside observers, such as speaking in tongues, can be misunderstood. We know that glossolalia (speaking in tongues) has been a practice of the Church since Apostolic times and has experienced a revival today, reaching into most of the Christian communions. Sometimes it has been associated with spiritual healing, because those who speak in tongues believe in healing. Spiritual healing is something that is separate and distinct from glossolalia, even though both gifts come from the same Spirit. However, I have known some people to be "turned off" by the practice of glossolalia through a lack of understanding and teaching regarding its use.

Where there is a good chance of alienating others and making a healing ministry more difficult to accept, it would be wise to use speaking in tongues in healing services only in those places where it has become a normal part of the worship experience of the congregation.

Along these lines it is sometimes helpful for visitors if the format of the service is printed on large cards for easy reading. The more we can eliminate feelings of strangeness from our healing service, the better it is for the uninstructed. In strictly denominational settings it matters little. People are familiar with their worship and hymn books and feel at ease with their own denominational services. As someone who was trained in a Congregational seminary to be a Methodist minister, finally ending up as an Episcopalian, I am especially conscious of how different liturgical services appear to those from a general Protestant background. The well ordered practices of the Episcopal church often come across as "sitting, kneeling, bobbing and weaving" to those attending for the first time.

These things apply to a lesser or greater degree to all denominational services and practices. If we do use them, it helps if we remember to make announcements that explain the differences to the visitors. When hymns are used, why not select those which are easy to sing and known by the majority of those present? You may pick out hymns which have an ideal message, but if nobody knows the tune they are so busy trying to figure out the music that they never do get the point of the words.

With all these things in mind, and having given some serious thought and prayer to what is best for your church or your community, you should be ready to launch your program. If you have made your preparations carefully, you should be able to proceed with a feeling of confidence and optimism. Final active preparations should consist of some teaching on the subject of spiritual healing, which includes an explanation of a healing service. The people should know the purpose of such a service and the function of the prayer group and the loving congregation. They should know the meaning of the laying-on-of-hands and how it is given. That is also true of Holy Unction or annointing. By the time you give these final instructions, you should have determined the place, day and time, for the healing services so that this information can be announced in advance. When you have completed this, all systems point to "GO."

Now, while the "count-down" is going on let us look at our check-list to make sure we have covered everything.

Ourselves: Are we personally ready? Have we read the Holy Scriptures and, from them, determined that we have been sent forth to heal? Do we *really* believe? Are we prepared to let God use us as He sees fit in carrying out this ministry?

Loving Congregation: Do we have the makings of this loving group, who will serve as our back-up and energy supply? Do we have those who *believe,* who will join with us in praying for the sick and assist us in our worship?

The Service: Have we chosen the format which will best suit the needs of our situation? Have we made sure that the service will contain within it the elements of prayer, Holy Scripture, penitence, and forgiveness, intercessions for the sick, teaching on the healing ministry, the opportunity to witness and share the good news of healings, sacramental acts of healing for those present, such as the laying-on-of-hands and annointing, and finally the opportunity for thanksgiving?

Right Climate: If we have taken care of the previous items we know that we have all the proper ingredients for the kind of climate in which healing may flourish. We may not be immediately aware of the results of our efforts but in time we may be assured that this will be known.

We are now ready for the "blast-off" which will launch us into a ministry which is highly relevant and personal to all who are involved. It is one aspect of our total ministry which strengthens our faith as we come face-to-face with the miraculous healing power of God.

Now that the program has begun there is one more thing required of you—*consistency.* You must be faithful to the program, even though it may seem to be moving slowly. It requires patience and faithfulness to build a strong and permanent healing ministry. I remember, earlier in my life, having a healing mission for five nights where there was no evidence of healing to be seen at any service. There were only small groups of people in attendance and when it ended I experienced a let-down feeling. I could see no way to measure the success or failure of the mission. I suppose I was really waiting for someone to leave his crutches at the altar rail. That would have been tangible evidence for me. Weeks and months later, however, seeds planted during that mission began to bear fruit as individuals who had been there let me know how they had been helped. In another situation where I wanted to start healing services, I had to ask my wife to go to the first service so I would be sure of having a congregation there. Eventually it grew into an effective group.

In the average clergyman's ministry the greatest number of healing experiences will take place with individuals apart from the service. You are called to the hospital to see the sick person. You are usually alone with the patient when you minister to him. But when you have the back-up assistance of a prayer group you are never alone. At the regular service you tell them how their prayer fortified you when you were with "Jim," for whom they had been praying. Often prayer groups all over the country join together praying for one sick person and that united prayer power backs up the doctors, nurses, and ministers who are caring for the patient.

That is why it is important to organize a prayer group and maintain regular healing services in each community. In these times when the average clergyman is trying to be involved in so many different areas of responsibility, the lay people of the Church must exert their own ministry. Clergy and laity alike have been commissioned to serve and when they both do their part the total ministry is strengthened.

Behind us all is He who sent us forth: Jesus, the Christ, the Son of the Living God.

XII.
You Can Heal

In the early church it was accepted that there was a diversity of gifts shared by the members, and that among those shared was the gift of healing. Throughout the centuries, as Christianity spread into all the world, the healing gifts continued to be received. All of us have within us the potential for healing. It is true then, that you can heal, or more precisely, that *God can heal through you.*

On the previous pages I have cited a variety of examples of God's healing. Most of those examples were observed by me in the normal course of my pastoral ministry. Other instances were reported to me by those directly involved, either as healer or recipient. Some cases reported as healings were without the involvement of a physician. Others made use of doctors, medicines, or surgery, in addition to spiritual means. In no case was the opportunity to retain the services of a physician denied or discouraged from anyone mentioned. In those cases without a doctor, the healing was so spontaneous that his services were never needed.

Though it is not difficult for me to believe in the reality of spiritual healing, because of what I have seen, it remains as a clouded issue among the general populace in our time. I do not believe that I have ever seen a television drama or a motion picture involving spiritual healing (with the exception of Biblical movies) that did not cast doubt on, or completely discredit, the healer as a charlatan. Time after time the story begins with a situation involving an unsuspecting patient, usually rich, who is being treated by some kind of "healer." Concerned family members and friends, suspicious of this kind of therapy, begin to investigate the "healer's" background and methods. As the plot comes to its conclusion the "healer" is exposed as a fraud and finally the patient is restored to health by an operation or other medical assistance.

On the one hand, these dramatic productions perform a genuine service, by alerting the public to the presence of actual charlatans who are at work in the world. The unfortunate aspect of this kind of show is the reflection it casts upon legitimate spiritual healings and prayer therapy.

How then is the average person to know the difference between the phoney healers and those who are genuine? What circumstances will make believers out of the multitude of doubters not only outside, but also within, the church?

The old saying, "the proof of the pudding is in the eating," applies in this case. We can believe if we can experience something outselves. It may be that we have personally been healed of illness. It could be the healing of a friend, which we have witnessed. The belief in healing might come from someone else's believing which has been shared with us.

But the most obvious reason for belief comes from the healing which resulted from your own actions. You prayed. You laid hands on someone who was sick—maybe your child, maybe your friend—and because of that, he was restored to health. In a case like that, the action is very definite, very fast—like *right now*. You laid your hands on a feverish head. An instant later the fever was gone. You placed your hand on a back, racked with pain. While your hand still rested there the sick person cried out, "the pain has gone!" Then you believe.

Yes, whether you are one the the clergy or a layman, male or female, old or young, you may be God's instrument for healing at any given time.

Again, before we continue further, let me digress for a moment to make a point clear. I am not trying to build a case for doing away with doctors. I believe in what the people in medicine are doing. I have confidence in my own physician, and call upon him when I have medical problems. All my family members have been under the regular care of family doctors since they were born. They received their regular immunizations and had their yearly checkups. The same was true concerning dental care, where we all received both preventive and remedial treatments. When someone in my family became ill, I would offer prayers and give the laying-on-of-hands. If the illness persisted or seemed to be getting worse, I consulted our family doctor. Calling the doctor did not mean that I had "tossed in the sponge" on spiritual healing. It only meant that I brought in another one of God's healers to help with the job. Naturally, my prayers did not cease when I brought the physician into the scene.

However, there were many occasions when I never needed to give the doctor a call. The laying-on-of-hands brought a quick halt to the fever or pain. The symptoms would subside. Health would be restored. Through the years, as my two daughters were growing up, prayer therapy was regularly used in our home.

"Dad, you'd better give me the laying-on-of-hands—my throat is sore." "Dad, give me the laying-on-of-hands—I have a headache."

When my wife, Joan, was ill with cancer she never required a shot for pain throughout the entire course of her illness. She only required two prescriptions for pain pills classified as narcotics and then used only one of them. The second bottle was kept on hand, "just in case I really need them." It was never used. Outside of aspirin, the laying-on-of-hands was all she ever required for relief from pain, and that relief lasted all night long.

Because it was a common practice in our home, everyone

in the family eventually came to use the laying-on-of-hands in all cases of sickness in the home. Of course, the hamsters and the cats became the first recipients of this at the hands of my daughters. Usually, as the family head and the most practiced one, I did the praying in cases of human illness. However, when I was not at home it became my wife's task, and now, as young mothers, it has become the practice of the girls.

I was pleased to learn that they have been able to use the laying-on-of-hands as a genuine source of help in the healing and comfort of their own children. Before starting with this chapter I consulted them both to see if they could give me any specifics on how they have benefitted from this recently.

"Why, just the other day, Kevin was screaming with pain in both ears—the doctor finally had to lance them. I just grabbed him to me and explained to him that I was going to put my hands on his ears and God would take away the pain, and when I did it he fell asleep in my arms—*right away!*"

My other daughter related that she too considered this a normal course of action in her home. As specific cases, she mentioned two things which stood out in her mind. While she and her husband were on vacation one of the children in the home they were visiting became ill. When my daughter heard crying in the bedroom, she stepped in and laid her hands upon his hot head and said a prayer. He stopped crying. About five minutes later he appeared in the room and said he was hungry. They touched his head and could tell that the fever had left. The other thing important to her children was the healing of their dog, Tinkerbell. Not long after she was adopted from the City Pound the little puppy became ill. They took him to a veterinarian, who, upon learning that he was a foundling, said that he probably had contracted distemper and there wasn't anything he could do about it. So the whole family began a therapy of love and prayer. And you know it already—Tinkerbell recovered. She always uses prayer with the children when they are sick.

"Whenever the children are sick I go in with them at night

and lay my hands on them. They usually fall right to sleep as I am praying for them and most always are better in the morning."

The ordained clergy have no corner on healing. Through the years laymen have figured prominently in the healing movement. Women have often been particularly gifted as teachers, writers, and healers as evidenced today by the many women who write on the subject. One thinks of Agnes Sanford, with her famous *Healing Light* and other works, and of Emily Gardiner Neal, who has written several books on healing. There is Kathryn Kuhlman and her writings and ministry. There are books by Rebecca Beard and Anne White. And let us not forget the late Ethel Tulloch Banks, who with her husband, was a founder of the Order of Saint Luke. Finally, though I do not subscribe to her rationale on the subject of healing, it would not be fair to omit the name of Mary Baker Eddy from any list of women involved in healing, for her Christian Science movement has undoubtedly been responsible for countless healings since its inception. Women are much in evidence in prayer groups at work throughout the church and the world; they share mightily in the total healing ministry.

In my own parishes I have always taught that God uses any of us for his different ministries; when some laymen take that to heart, they find themselves actually functioning as ministers of healing.

"I have to tell you, Father, Bob has received the gift of healing. He laid hands on our daughter-in-law when she was so sick and she was healed. Isn't that wonderful?"

"Yes, Father, I did what you said and prayed for my little girl's wart condition. I'll be darned if they didn't go away."

"I was visiting my friend in the hospital, and the woman in the next bed to his was moaning and groaning with pain. I remembered what you said about the laying-on-of-hands and tried it out, and it worked. Almost as soon as I touched her, she calmed down and went right to sleep."

All these were testimonies of laymen who were prompted to act as God's ministers of concern and healing. I remember a story involving a group of laymen, told to me by a woman living in rural Maine.

"Once I was so sick the doctor had given me up for dead. My neighbor lady asked my husband if she could bring some of her church members by to pray for me. He wasn't too sure he wanted that—they were Pentecostals, I think—then he thought how sick I was and decided it wouldn't hurt any, so he let them in. Well, they came in and knelt around my bed, and someone was speaking in tongues, and while all this was going on I had a vision of a hand coming down and touching me—it was no human hand. When I felt it touch me I began to feel good, and I knew I was going to get better."

Again the people who gathered around the bed were laymen. I talked about this incident with the local doctor and he backed up the story, affirming that in his estimation the woman had been dying and that after the Pentecostals had been there her healing was rapid.

I have mentioned only a few cases that have come to my attention, but what of the great majority of personal healings that are never brought to light? When Agnes Sanford points out that the laying-on-of-hands as an instinctive act ("What mother has not soothed a crying baby with the laying-on of hands"[1]) done by virtually all mothers at one time or another, we realize that the number of answered prayers can only be measured in astronomical figures. If we can give people a proper approach, proper intentions, and knowledge of their healing potential, far more persons may benefit from spiritual healing.

When we think of ourselves performing acts of healing it may seem presumptuous to us. Who are we to assume such authority? When we analyze the whole situation and realize that we are merely the pipeline from God to the patient, it becomes more acceptable. After all, hasn't God always used people to carry out his will? Agnes Sanford makes our role in healing very clear:

> Christ is the healer. No human being has power to heal.
> Christ loves all of us, and sends His love through us to
> His children according to His will. If we quiet ourselves
> and let Him speak we will not go wrong. His love not
> only directs us to those whom He would heal, but also
> directs every word that we say and everything that we
> do.[2]

With that assurance behind us, we should be more ready to
proceed, knowing that we shall be directed all the way.
Around other adults we might not wish to act for fear of
what they might think. However, with children we have a
good place to start, for they do not look upon prayer, or
healing, as strange. They accept it as a most natural thing.

What better place can we find to introduce healing prayer
than our own home, with our own family? And what better
time than when we join with the children for their evening
prayers? If a friend or relative is ill, let that be a part of the
family prayers. When one of the family members is sick, use
the laying-on-of-hands as a regular part of the evening
prayers. Also use it spontaneously whenever someone is hurt
or suddenly gets sick. As soon as you put them to bed, lay
hands on them and pray aloud for their recovery. As Mrs.
Sanford says, He will direct "every word that we say and
everything that we do."

If we have doubts about what to do, remember the
rationale about healing. We start with God. He is the Father
of us all, who made us for Himself and wants us well. He is
the source of all energy, light, and power, all the elements
necessary to bring life and health to the sick. He is the
transmitter. You are the receiver. Because of your
belief—because you are willing to be His servant, His
messenger—He will send His power into you and through you
to the one who is sick.

With this knowledge in mind, you approach the sick
person and minister to him in the way that comes naturally
to you. You have to remain "loose," ready to move in the

way God is guiding you. Keep in mind that love and compassion are the keys to your own readiness to transmit God's healing to the sick person. Look upon the patient as the child of God, loved by the same Father who will be working in you to restore him to health.

Your thoughts must be away from yourself; they must center around the goodness and absolute power of God. By submerging your own self, your ego, your desires, and allowing God's being and presence to dominate the scene, you can more perfectly obey His will. In doing that you overcome such weaknesses as indecision and doubt. You also overcome any self-consciousness you may have had about healing ministrations.

Tell the sick person what you are there for and what you expect will happen. Let him know how God can make him well. Tell him you believe that, and that is why you are there to pray for his healing. As you pray for him, make a mental picture of him as God sees him, strong, happy, and healthy.

As you finish your prayer, be sure to add a note of thanksgiving. It is something you'll want to do anyway, when you realize how wonderful it is that God is using you for this good purpose. You'll want to say "thanks" as you feel the gratitude of the patient and that of his family. Again, you'll want to fall on your knees in grateful praise when they inform you that the patient has been restored to health. "Rejoice always, pray constantly, give thanks in all circumstances; for this is the will of God in Christ Jesus for you" (I Thessalonians 5:16, R.S.V.).

There are some guidelines you can offer the sick person, aids that will assist him in his recovery. From the writings and practices of a number of authorities in the field of spiritual healing and psychology, we get some of the same suggestions for gaining health in body, mind, and spirit. Virtually all suggest setting aside a regular time each day to meditate, pray, and think positively about the future.

First make sure that the sick person is comfortable

andrelaxed.. See that he frees himself from other distractions such as television and radio. In the hospital, he can ask the nurse to keep him from other interruptions during his quiet time.

Whenever we need power, we must seek out the *source.* That is where we start out with our meditation. To help us to keep our thoughts in the right direction we should avail ourselves of the Scriptures as well as other inspirational writings. Choose something simple—not too wordy or complicated.

After starting out with our thoughts on God and His power, we can then ask that same power to enter into us and give us life and health. This we know he *can* do. In time this we know he *will* do.

The next thing we must learn is an exercise, highly valued by such diverse persons as Harry Emerson Fosdick, Glen Clark, Leslie Weatherhead, Agnes Sanford, and the physician who wrote *Psycho-Cybernetics,* Maxwell Maltz. Each one of these persons recommends the use of the imagination in visual exercises, where you come to see yourself in a new and better light.

Agnes Sanford says, "Make a picture on your mind of your body well."[3] In Glen Clark's course on spiritual healing,[4] he uses visualization exercises as healing techniques, along with reading exercises, meditation exercises, memorizing exercises, and prayer exercises. Though Dr. Maltz is writing specifically about the problem of building a new self-image, his suggestions are similar. He gets the person to stop looking at himself as defeated or weak, and has him seeing himself—in his imagination—as he wants to be:

Imagine how you would feel if you were already the sort of personality you want to be. If you have been shy and timid, see yourself moving among people with ease and poise—and *feeling good* because of it. If you have been fearful and anxious in certain situations—see yourself acting calmly and deliberately, acting with confidence and courage—and feeling expansive and confident because you are.[5]

Because many physically sick persons also have mental and emotional problems, they would also benefit emotionally from a change in self image. Isn't that what happens as the result of conversion, of being "born again," and coming forth with a new personality as a child of God? When the sick person can see his new self-image as that of a vibrant, useful, and restored person, he contributes to his own healing processes. That is one way he can cooperate with God in gaining new life and health. He now sees himself in the kind of self-image any Christian should have, because through Christ he has been made strong in the Lord, because the Holy Spirit dwells within him, because he is Christ's soldier and servant.

You can teach those who are sick to use these practices after you have given them your healing ministrations. Even though some persons recover immediately, such cases are rare. As a result, most of the seriously ill are confined to the hospital or home. Even those who are ambulatory and come to our healing services have time on their hands when they can use these daily periods for relaxing and putting into practice prayer, meditation, and visualization exercises. You can prescribe this quiet time as a daily tonic and tell the patient that you expect him to do his part in the process.

Yes, *you can heal.* God can make you the instrument that will bring new life to another person. He can use you to bring light where there has been darkness, courage where there has been fear, hope where there has been despair, and new life instead of death. It is a part of the commission you received when you were baptized, to "fight under his banner against sin, the world, and the devil; and to continue Christ's faithful soldier and servant unto [your] life's end." It is the command that sends you forth to tell the good news and to *heal the sick.*

Footnotes

Chapter II

[1]Glen Clark, *Be Thou Made Whole,* (St. Paul, Minn: Macalester Park, 1953), p. 148.

Chapter III

[1]Bernard Martin, *The Healing Ministry in the Church,* (Richmond, Va.: John Knox Press, 1960), p. 12.

[2]*Book of Common Prayer,* from "The Order for the Visitation of the Sick," p. 316.

[3]*Manual of Christian Healing of the Order of St. Luke,* 12th Edition. John Gaynor Banks, 2243 Front St., San Diego, Calif. 92101: St. Luke's Press, 1953, p. 34.

[4]Emily Gardiner Neal, *Where There's Smoke,* (Wilton, Conn.: Morehouse-Barlow Co., 1967), pp. 37-38.

[5]*Ibid,* p. 30.

Chapter IV

[1]Wade H. Boggs, Jr., *Faith Healing and the Christian Faith,* (Richmond, Va.: John Knox Press, 1956).

[2]Don H. Gross, *The Case for Spiritual Healing,* (New York: Thomas Nelson & Sons, 1958).

[3]Bernard Martin, *The Healing Ministry in the Church,* (Richmond, Va.: John Knox Press, 1960), p. 52.

[4]Richard C. Cabot and Russell L. Dicks, *The Art of Minister-*

ing to the Sick, (New York: The Macmillan Co., 1936).
⁵Russell L. Dicks, *Pastoral Work and Personal Counseling,*
(New York: The Macmillan Co., 1964), p. 164.

Chapter V

¹Glen Clark, *Be Thou Made Whole,* (St. Paul, Minn.: Macalester Park, 1953), p. 148.
²John Ellis Large, *The Ministry of Healing,* (Wilton, Conn.:
Morehouse-Barlow Co., 1959), p. 107. Abridged edition,
The Church and Healing, available from Forward Movement
Publications, Cincinnati, Ohio.
³Emily Gardiner Neal, *Where There's Smoke,* (Wilton,
Conn.: Morehouse-Barlow Co., 1967), p. 45.
⁴Agnes Sanford, *The Healing Light,* (St. Paul, Minn.: Macalester Park, 1947), p. 28.
⁵Alfred W. Price, *Religion and Health,* Philadelphia: St.
Stephen's Church, n.d.), p. 14.
⁶Agnes Sanford, *The Healing Light,* (St. Paul, Minn.: Macalester Park, 1947), p. 28.
⁷John Ellis Large, *The Ministry of Healing,* (Wilton, Conn.:
Morehouse-Barlow, Co., 1959), p. 179.
⁸Howard J. Clinebell, Jr., *Understanding and Counseling the
Alcoholic,* (Nashville, Tenn.: Abingdon Press, 1956), p. 234.
Ibid., p. 235.

Chapter VI

¹*Manual of Christian Healing of the Order of St. Luke,* 12th
Edition, 1962. John Gaynor Banks, 2243 Front St., San
Diego, Calif. 92101: St. Luke's Press, 1953, p. 3.
²Leslie D. Weatherhead, *Prescription for Anxiety,* (Nashville
Tenn.: Abingdon Press, 1956), p. 67.

Chapter VII

[1]William L. Carrington, M.D., *The Healing of Marriage,* Channel Press, N.Y., 1961, p. 13.
[2]Emily Gardiner Neal, *Where There's Smoke,* (Wilton, Conn.: Morehouse-Barlow Co., 1967), pp. 17-18.

Chapter IX

[1]Emily Gardiner Neal, *A Reporter Finds God Through Spiritual Healing,* (Wilton, Conn.: Morehouse-Barlow Co., 1956).
[2]Emily Gardiner Neal, *Where There's Smoke,* (Wilton, Conn.: Morehouse-Barlow Co., 1967), p. 115.

Chapter XI

[1]John Ellis Large, *The Ministry of Healing,* (Wilton, Conn.: Morehouse-Barlow Co., 1959), p. 71.

Chapter XII

[1]Agnes Sanford, *The Healing Light,* (St. Paul, Minn.: Macalester Park, 1947), p. 31.
[2]*Ibid,* p. 114.
[3]*Ibid,* p. 37.
[4]Glen Clark, *Be Thou Made Whole,* (St. Paul, Minn.: Macalester Park, 1953).
[5]Maxwell Maltz, *Psycho-Cybernetics,* (Englewood Cliffs: Prentice Hall, 1960), p. 42.

Bibliography

Beard, Rebecca, *Everyman's Search*. Wells, Vt., Merrybrook
Press, 1950. A medical doctor's involvement with spiritual healing.

Boggs, Wade H., Jr., *Faith Healing and the Christian Faith*.
Richmond, Va., John Knox Press, 1956. A work sharply
critical of faith healing, emphasizing that spiritual growth
and character development often come from illness and
suffering.

Cabot, Richard C., and Russell L. Dicks, *The Art of Ministering to the Sick*. New York, The Macmillan Co., 1936.
The role of minister as visitor and chaplain to the sick,
working in cooperation with the doctor and hospital
staff.

Carrington, William L., *The Healing of Marriage*. Port
Washington, N.Y., Channel Press, 1961. A practical aid
for the marriage counselor.

Clark, Glenn, *Be Thou Made Whole*. St. Paul, Minn., Macalester Park Press, 1953. A helpful book giving step-by-
step procedures for achieving a healthful life.

       , *How to Find Health Through Prayer*. New
York, Harper & Brothers, 1940. Practical suggestions
about living the healthy life.

Clinebell, Howard J., Jr., *Understanding and Counseling the
Alcoholic*. Nashville, Tenn., Abingdon Press, 1956.

Gives some history along with practical suggestions for counseling the alcoholic through the combined use of religion and psychology.

Dicks, Russell L., *Pastoral Work and Personal Counseling.* New York, The Macmillan Co., 1949. A guidebook for ministers.

Gross, Don H., *The Case for Spiritual Healing.* New York, Thomas Nelson & Sons, 1958. A survey of the revival of spiritual healing, an answer to critics, and a positive presentation of the role of the Church in healing.

Large, John Ellis, *The Ministry of Healing.* Wilton, Conn., Morehouse-Barlow Co., 1959. (Abridged edition, *The Church and Healing.* Cincinnati, Ohio, Forward Movement Publications, 1965). A thoughtful and well expressed appraisal of healing in the Church with practical suggestions for uses in the local parish.

Martin, Bernard, *The Healing Ministry in the Church.* Richmond, Va., John Knox Press, 1960. A biblically oriented study of the Church's healing ministry that places a responsibility on today's ministers to hearken to the commands of the Lord.

Neal, Emily Gardiner, *A Reporter Finds God Through Spiritual Healing.* Wilton, Conn., Morehouse-Barlow Co., 1956. A personal account of the author's awakening to the realities of spiritual healing after having approached the subject as a skeptic.

———, *Where There's Smoke.* Wilton, Conn., Morehouse-Barlow Co., 1967. As in her earlier book, Mrs. Neal appeals to the doubter and also gives much help to the believer in this account of her further experiences with spiritual healing.

Oates, Wayne, E., ed., *An Introduction to Pastoral Counseling.* Nashville, Tenn., Broadman Press, 1959. A joint effort by a group of professors of pastoral counseling, this is a helpful introduction to the subject for ministers, with many practical suggestions.

Oursler, Will, *The Healing Power of the Faith.* New York, Hawthorne Books, 1957. A well written account of spiritual healing as practiced in various parts of Christendom today.

Rogers, Carl R., *Counseling and Psychotherapy.* Boston, Houghton-Mifflin Co., 1942. A careful guide to counseling by a leading psychologist. It can be of immeasurable assistance to a minister engaged in pastoral counseling.

Sanford, Agnes, *The Healing Light.* St. Paul, Minn., Macalester Park Press, 1947. One of the best-known books on the healing ministry, it shows how laymen can be actively involved in healing and offers many practical suggestions for use in everyday situations. One of several books by the same author.

Scherzer, Carl J., *The Church and Healing.* Philadelphia, Westminster Press, 1950. An overall history of healing in the Church, in which all kinds of healing and healers are treated objectively.

Steward, Charles William, *The Minister as Marriage Counselor.* Nashville, Tenn., Abingdon Press, 1961. A discussion of the role-relationship theory of counseling, helpful for an understanding of the counseling process. This book shows how the minister can function effectively as a counselor, and at the same time recognizes a minister's limitations in that field.

Manual of Christian Healing of the Order of St. Luke, 12th Edition. San Diego, Calif., Order of Saint Luke, 1962. Edited by John Gaynor Banks, founder of the Order, this is the official manual for members. Among other things, it explains the theological basis for spiritual healing and includes forms for different kinds of ministrations and services.

Sharing. A monthly magazine published in behalf of the Order of Saint Luke, 2243 Front St., San Diego, Calif. Contains articles on spiritual healing, book reviews, and announcements of special events such as conferences on healing. Offers an inter-denominational directory of available healing services and maintains a complete listing of books and pamphlets on spiritual healing.